Bending Heaven

BENDING HEAVEN

stories by

Jessica Francis Kane

COUNTERPOINT

WASHINGTON, D.C.

Portions of this book have appeared previously in the following magazines: "How to Become a Publicist," *The Missouri Review;* "Paris," *Salt Hill;* "Pantomime," *The C-Ville Weekly;* "Exposure," *Virginia Quarterly Review;* "The Arnold Proof," *Michigan Quarterly Review.* The author thanks these magazines and their editors.

Library of Congress Cataloging-in-Publication Data
Kane, Jessica Francis, 1971-
Bending heaven : stories / Jessica Francis Kane.
p. cm.
ISBN 1-58243-206-6 (alk. paper)
1. United States—Social life and customs—20th century—Fiction. 2. London (England)—Social life and customs—Fiction. I. Title.
PS3611.A76 B46 2002
813'.6—dc21

2001007345

FIRST PRINTING

Jacket and text design by Gopa & Ted2

COUNTERPOINT
P.O. Box 65793
Washington, D.C. 20035–5793

Counterpoint is a member of the Perseus Books Group

10 9 8 7 6 5 4 3 2 1

For my mother and father,

and for Mitchell

If Heaven I cannot bend,
then Hell I will arouse.

Virgil, The Aeneid,
Book VII

Contents

Evidence of Old Repairs   11

How to Become a Publicist   31

Refuge   48

Paris   71

Ideas of Home,
but Not the Thing Itself   76

First Sale   90

Pantomime   106

Exposure   114

The Trailing Spouse   138

Wreckers   156

The Arnold Proof   173

Acknowledgments   199

Evidence of Old Repairs

THEIR FIRST MORNING in London, a Monday, Sarah looked out the window and saw a squirrel eating from a woman's hand. Their hotel, the Royal Lancaster, stood on the north edge of Hyde Park. It was the middle of February, off-season, the only way they could afford to come, and the reason, Sarah believed, that they'd been given a room on such a high floor with windows facing south. These rooms went for much more in the summer, she was sure. They had a beautiful view over the Italian fountains at the top of the Serpentine and the park stretching away to the left and right. The landscape looked as though it had been drawn overnight in wet ink, the grass a moist dark green, the bare trees blackened by rain. Even the woman kneeling down to the squirrel was wearing a slick yellow raincoat that looked shiny and fresh.

Sarah shook her head in wonder. They had never had a room with such a view. In her life, she had rarely felt taller than the trees.

She called to her daughter. She thought Amelia would like to see that the squirrels were so tame.

Amelia, already up and dressed and reading at the table in the corner of the room, did not look up. "I'm reading," she said.

Sarah let the curtain fall closed and watched her. She was

thirteen and pretty in a girlish way, not like some of her friends who already looked grown-up. She played the violin, seriously and well, and had an enviable sense of confidence. She was beginning to enter Michigan state competitions and Sarah, sick with nerves in the audience, marveled at the self-possession she exhibited when she walked onto the stage. Other times, though, when Sarah watched her unaware, walking up the block from school or standing in the driveway waiting for a friend, this same calm manifested itself in a stillness, a quiet wariness that worried her.

"Any time you guys are ready," Amelia said, turning a page.

It was ten o'clock and her father was in the shower and Sarah was still in her robe. They'd said on the plane that they would try to get an early start each morning; they only had one week. But Sarah and Mark had been exhausted when the wake-up call came at eight. Amelia, however, had jumped out of bed. It was her spring break and her first time abroad.

"There are some squirrels eating out of a woman's hand in the park." Sarah turned back to the window and pulled the curtains wide open. This, as she had hoped, Amelia could not resist. She had always loved animals and that seemed not to have changed. She put down her book and came over.

"Down there." Sarah pointed. "On the left side of the water, past the fountains. See?"

Amelia nodded. "They're coming right to her hand. I wonder what she's feeding them."

"We could try it later. Would you like that?"

"Sure."

Sarah tried to see her expression, but Amelia kept her face turned to the park.

What Sarah tried to remember is whether Amelia had had

this stillness before. She'd been a good baby, never too fussy, and as a young child could play happily by herself for hours. From the day she entered school she'd been an excellent student, apparently motivated by an inner need to achieve. Still, Sarah was sometimes sure that there had been a spark in her eye, an easier laughter, that was now gone.

Mark came out of the bathroom. He was dressed and combing his hair. "All yours," he said to Sarah. Then, quietly, as she walked past him, "How are you?"

He was referring, she knew, to the fact that she'd had a drink on the plane. "Fine," she answered, trying to warm the coldness out of her voice. She was scared of flying, and anyway it had been almost four months since she had last had too much. "And you? How did you sleep?"

"Like a log," he said, kissing her on the cheek.

———

Sarah and Mark had come through a bad time after she discovered his affair, a year of silent dinners and midnight arguments. The affair was already over when she learned of it, and Mark had been the one to end it—of that she was certain. He swore it had been a mistake, that he was still in love with her. He was as committed as ever to the marriage, he said, and this did seem to be true. He proposed therapy, a suggestion that surprised her because he was such a private man, and a few months later the sessions seemed to come to a natural, satisfactory conclusion. The counselor, beaming at them on the day of their final meeting, told them they were one of his greatest successes. "Go into the world and love each other," he said, flinging his arms wide as they left his office. The motion, combined with all his beneficence, made Sarah feel they should have been a pair of white doves flying out of a bag. She very nearly flapped her arms, but Mark took her elbow and guided her out of the building. It was spring and everything seemed back on track. They took down the storm windows and put up the screens. The daffodil bulbs she'd planted by the garage sent up clusters of green shoots. Then one evening—making julienne salad for dinner and waiting for Amelia to come home from her violin lesson and Mark to come home from the office—Sarah poured a shot of rum into her Pepsi. This in itself was not unusual, but tonight, sipping the cocktail, slicing the ham and cheese for the salad, the rum seemed to loosen the hold she had on herself. She poured another. Her mother had been an alcoholic, her grandmother one as well. Did this explain Sarah's problems? Sarah didn't think so, despite all the rhetoric of the age. She poured another drink. Two hours later the salad was a soggy confetti instead of the elegant strips it was meant to be and Sarah, looking deep into the white plastic bowl, knew this was a metaphor for her. She was in tears when Amelia and Mark came home, but on that night and the ones that followed, she was easily able to conceal what was happening. The fact of the matter was, she didn't drink that much. She never stumbled or slurred. She never got angry or abusive. And she never stopped doing any of the things they expected of her—laundry, shopping, cooking, cleaning. She just drank and got sad.

In the lobby, Sarah asked about the squirrels. Was feeding allowed? The concierge, kind but distant, with a smile that suggested pity rather than camaraderie, said it was not recom-

mended but that it was not illegal; it was, in fact, quite a popular activity with the tourists, feeding the squirrels in Hyde
Park. He went on to say that this time of year they could also
see bunnies, geese, coots, moorhens, and magpies. It was too
late for the mandarin duck and too early for the cygnets, two
more favorites with the tourists. He held out a list of wildlife
commonly spotted in London's parks, which Sarah thought
Amelia would take, as she was the one interested in animals.
But Amelia and Mark had taken several steps away from the
desk, and Sarah had to spin to find them, her purse strap slipping off her shoulder.

"Come on, Mom," Amelia said, taking her father's hand.

Sarah turned back to the concierge. She had never been able
to be rude. "Thank you," she said, taking the sheet of paper. The
man bowed.

"He was making fun of you," Amelia said when they were
out on the street.

"Yes, well," said Sarah. "What was I supposed to do?"

Probably no one ever would have found out. Sarah would have
pulled herself together eventually, would have regained the control she felt she had almost intentionally surrendered. She was
already having an easier time getting up in the morning and taking walks in the afternoon for exercise. But one day Amelia came
home from school and took a sip of Sarah's Pepsi. It was sitting
on the counter by the kitchen sink, in the tall water glass Sarah
always used.

"Mom?" she called.

Sarah had gone to the front door to get the mail. She'd only left the kitchen for a minute, but Amelia's orchestra rehearsal had been canceled and she'd come in the side door. She must have been thirsty; her violin case was still slung over her shoulder.

"What's in this?"

"I'm having a cocktail," Sarah answered calmly. It was three o'clock in the afternoon.

"I don't believe this." Amelia looked at the floor, then quickly up again. "This is why you never share your drinks with me."

Sarah thought hard, but there didn't seem to be anything to say. It was true. She watched Amelia, who stood quietly watching her, seemingly replaying the previous weeks in light of this new information, questioning and judging everything that had been slightly out of the ordinary or difficult to understand. Coming to the end, to the ill-fated sip, she said again, "I don't believe this," and ran upstairs to her room.

Sarah imagined that ever after soda would be for Amelia what madeleines were for Proust, opening up whole chapters of memory, most of them painful. And the irony of it all was the timing. A few years earlier, her little pigtailed Amelia would have simply spat the mouthful into the sink and told her mother the soda had gone bad. A few years later, she might have smiled conspiratorially and asked if she could have one, too. But, at thirteen, Amelia was being subjected to a series of anti-drug classes at school that left her believing mood-altering substances of any kind slicked the road to hell. Sarah and Mark had always enjoyed a glass of wine with dinner. Now this was nearly impossible. They sipped desultorily while Amelia harangued them with her latest facts and figures. "Did you know," she had said one evening, "that an alcoholic can be defined as anyone who uses alcohol habitually?" From her chair at the side of the table, she turned left and right, raising an eyebrow at each of them, opposing players in the tennis match of her life. "Well, what I see here, a glass of wine every night, is a habit."

And on this particular night, Amelia turned to her father before her first bite. Mark raised his wineglass in a mock toast to the evening lecture he believed was about to begin. Sarah, breathing slowly, stared at the store-bought peonies in the center of the table. It was odd how, even at this moment, she was proud of the arrangement she'd made.

"Something's wrong," Amelia said, her voice surprisingly timid.

They stood together on the north bank of the Serpentine; more accurately, Sarah now knew from studying the map at Lancaster Gate, the Long Water. She had pointed this out to Amelia and Mark.

"Long Water?" Mark said.

Tracing the map with her finger, Sarah started to say how the water was, in fact, if you looked at it, a long narrow shape before widening into the more irregular Serpentine, but Amelia interrupted her.

"Deep water maybe," she said, looking at her father to see if he would think this funny.

"Good point," he said, smiling.

Pigeons and seagulls were gathering noisily around their feet, but the squirrels Amelia was coaxing with the bread crumbs remained at a distance, scurrying about under cover of the wild bank beyond the iron fence that edged the path. It was eleven o'clock, and the park was filled with slow runners and determined walkers. A few men and women in dark suits hurried by

with briefcases and portfolios, their heels rhythmically crunching the brown pebbled path, their long coats flapping open as
they walked. The air was cool, but the day was clear and the
sunshine offered a bit of meager warmth.

Mark had been surprised by the proposal to do this first
thing. He was ready with the guidebook, ready to see the British
Museum before lunch, the National Gallery after. But Sarah
had insisted and when Amelia didn't disagree, he conceded.
Now he stood a few steps away, just a bit up the incline where
the path curved gently to the left, his hands stuffed into the
pockets of his coat. Sarah knew he didn't want to be here, but
she also knew that he was wary of her, uncertain and therefore
less critical. Amelia crouched low on the path, ticking and clucking with her tongue, and Sarah stood right behind her, more
bread in her hand at the ready. She was enjoying herself.

Planting daffodils by the garage had turned out to be a bad
idea. It rained a lot that spring in Ann Arbor and the rain
turned the bed to mud, which splattered up onto the white wall
of the garage, and onto the long green daffodil leaves, and
finally onto the lemon-yellow flowers themselves.

There were scenes, at night usually, and music during the
afternoons. Rachmaninoff, Chopin, the Humming Chorus
from *Madama Butterfly* (oh and it was the wakeful night of her
soul, too), Lalo's *Symphonie Espagnole*. Sarah played them endlessly.

And Amelia, hearing the music, went straight to her room
after school. Often Sarah didn't see her until dinnertime, when
Mark came home.

She stood by the kitchen window, making dinner and think-

ing about Amelia above. She wondered if while trying to concentrate on her homework she was straining to hear the cabinet
at the end of the counter opening, the splash of liquid meeting
liquid. Probably she was. She thought about going out and trying to wipe off the muddy daffodils, but cleaning a flower
seemed like a strange and futile thing to do.

———

Each morning before their sight-seeing, Sarah guided them to
the same place on the east bank of the Long Water, where they
faced Peter Pan, the sprightly statue in the clearing across the
water. A straight line of mossy wooden moorings ran between
the two banks, occupied, usually, by brilliant white seagulls, one
to each pillar, while others soared overhead, vying for position.
Occasionally a few shiny black cormorants moved in and easily
commandeered a few spots on the row. It was a beautiful,
chaotic scene that suggested to Sarah much larger bodies of
water than a small lake in a park.

Remarkably, the seagulls, pigeons, and wood doves began to
recognize their little family by the third morning and gathered
quickly for their morning crumbs. This was noisy and exciting,
and for the first time Sarah understood why children and the
elderly love feeding the birds in parks. It was thrilling being the
center of so much fluttering attention. For the squirrels, she
collected rolls and crackers from their lunches. She ripped and
broke these into small pieces and kept them in a plastic bag in
her purse. The squirrels, however, would not take the food unless
Amelia put it on the ground, which she did, dispassionately.

"Mom, I don't think this is working," she said, standing up
and looking doubtfully at her mother.

Sarah was kneeling on the path, her arm extended through the fence up to the shoulder. "Don't worry," she answered, slightly breathless with the effort.

Amelia brushed off her pants and crouched again.

Sarah tried to think of everything she knew about squirrels. She'd visited Assateague once, a barrier island off the coast of Maryland and Virginia. The gray squirrel was endangered there and was being reintroduced. Boxes had been nailed to trees all over the island for them to nest in. At night, to check their population, park rangers went around with dim flashlights, lifting the roofs of the boxes and counting the sleeping squirrels inside. Each family had to be accounted for.

But what did squirrels eat?

It was Wednesday and Mark had brought a cup of coffee to the park. He was sitting on a bench nearby, hunched forward, sipping. He was watching them, his face pale and blank.

"Peanuts," Sarah said suddenly. "Amelia, tomorrow we'll try peanuts."

By the time the chrysanthemums in the side bed were in bloom (during a cold dry autumn that made the reds and oranges as vivid as Sarah had ever seen them), she understood Mark and Amelia's fears better than she did her own behavior, so it made sense to seek help. She went to AA, but after three weeks felt certain that her problem was not that of the classic alcoholic. She didn't fit the profile. Once before in her marriage she had had a bout of drinking, but after a few months stopped. Wasn't a real alcoholic permanently recovering, never allowed to have another drink? But she had gone back without a problem to having a glass of wine with dinner and even a cocktail or two at parties. AA referred her to ACA, Adult Children of Alcoholics, but this didn't help either. Same prayers, more blame, it seemed, and she didn't want to blame her mother; none of it felt like her fault. Once, when she was twenty-five or so and had finally assembled a few facts about her family, Sarah asked her mother, Margaret, why she'd never talked about the difficulties of her own childhood, her ordeals with her mother.

But Margaret just stared at her. "And when should I have told you about it?" she said. "Over which peanut-butter-and-jelly sandwich?"

She had always thought her mother's point a good one. It reminded her of something else she'd liked to say, "Let the problems of the day be sufficient unto the day." The same should be true for generations, her mother felt, and Sarah agreed. She gave up all acronyms and vowed to quit drinking again on her own. It was mid-October and, except for one night in November, she did.

———

Passing through the lobby on their fourth morning, Sarah noticed that the concierge smiled and gave a little salute in Amelia's direction. She turned quickly to see Amelia grin and wave back.

"Have you spoken to him?" she asked when they were outside. She couldn't keep it from sounding like an accusation.

Amelia stared, her eyes wide. "I asked him where to get the peanuts," she said.

In the park, several aggressive geese joined the melee, as well as a few mallard pairs with impeccable manners. Quiet and noble, they took what was within reach and left the frenzied hunting and pecking to others. The number of birds seemed to be a deterrent to the squirrels, so Sarah sent Amelia further down the path to try to lure the squirrels from the underbrush while she fed the birds in the clearing.

Mark, this morning, had brought a newspaper with his coffee. Amelia, hesitating before going to her post, appealed to him for help. He shook his head.

"I don't think so," he said. "This is your and your mother's thing."

Sarah demurred from where she was standing a few steps away. "Oh, come on, Mark," she said. "We're just feeding the animals here. You're welcome to join in." She sounded annoyed and turned to lob a piece of bread gently in the direction of a retiring female duck. It hit her on the head.

Mark smiled and looked at Amelia. "I don't think so," he said again and began to unfurl his newspaper.

"Right," Amelia said. "I understand."

Perhaps it was because the yard hadn't been raked all season. Or maybe because Sarah had woken flushed and irritable after a late nap on a gray November afternoon. She went outside to get some air, to try to cheer up, but standing by the garage she began surveying the back of the house, the yard, the neighboring houses, the other backyards. Little rectangular plots of land abutting the vulnerable backs of houses. Windy screened-in porches, peeling paint, thick black wires like spindly buttresses connecting everyone to the central nave of telephone poles running down the center of the block. Their own yard needed tending to, the garage painting. There was a honeysuckle bush that had been allowed to grow into a sort of tree with a trunk so off-center and twisted it had to be supported with a two-by-four. There was a hackberry by the side patio that was so storm-ravaged Sarah counted seven blunt branches where the tree had once stretched out into a lovely shape. It brought tears to her eyes, rising as it did in its broken, awkward way above their house.

The sky was pale blue, fading nearly to white in the east, and the sunset was obscured by a low, cluttered horizon of trees and houses. Music, an upbeat march punctuated by steady percussion, drifted to her from the direction of the stadium: the Michigan marching band practicing for the game that weekend. Ann Arbor suddenly seemed like a very small town, cross-hatched and cinched together by nothing more than telephone cables and marching bands.

That was when she decided to plan a trip to England. But she also decided, heading down the driveway toward the kitchen door, that she would have a drink to warm her and rake the yard.

They were amazing, they really were. Sometimes the two of them heard a high pitch that no one else could hear; sometimes their eardrums, more sensitive than most, were disturbed by a vibration that no one else could feel. They would look at each other quickly, checking to see if the other one felt it, too. Then they would plug their ears or rub them, shaking their heads together in smiling bewilderment.

When this happened in the restaurant in Piccadilly where they were having lunch on their fifth afternoon, Sarah put down her soup spoon and looked back and forth between them. "You two are just peas in a pod," she said.

"Mom, stop," said Amelia.

"What? It's true," she said. "You're very like your father, Amelia."

"Mom, we both have sensitive ears. It's no big deal."

"Oh, I think it is."

An argument might have started if it weren't for the music that came on in the restaurant just then. They all recognized it: Rachmaninoff's second piano concerto, one of Sarah's favorites, only in a terrible Hooked-on-Classics version with a steady beat in the background. It was like a parody of their family grief, the comic score in place of the tragic. It was so reminiscent for all of them of the dark months of Sarah's drinking that none of them knew what to say or where to look. This was not the first time music had united them in this way, engulfing them suddenly like an afternoon squall. And as on those other occasions, Sarah thought how this feeling, this mutual discomfort, was like a dark figure whom she had brought into their midst and now couldn't dismiss. She was astonished by the injustice. She had not done what Mark had done. She did not have his career or Amelia's talent. What she had was them, her family. How could she be the one who had caused the most damage?

It was drizzling when they left the restaurant. Mark stepped forward and opened one of their two umbrellas. Amelia started after him, but then stopped and turned. Someone watching might have missed the moment of indecision. She stepped quickly back up the curb and joined her mother under the second umbrella. It was an apology, Sarah knew, not a wish, but she took it, squeezing Amelia's arm.

Raking leaves. Because it was something Mark usually did, it had not occurred to Sarah that the job would include clearing the leaves out of the evergreen bushes that lined the front of the house. But dry yellow and brown leaves littered the top of the bushes, and some had nestled down into the dense dark green needles for the season. She worked with her hands until they were scratched and raw, then switched to the rake. It was a strange and wonderful thing, beating those bushes with the rake.

The morning of their last full day was still and white. A low mist the color of the sky skirted the trees in the park. It was warmer than it had been all week and smells from blocks away—fish, burning coffee, diesel fumes—hung in the air in pockets. The surface of the water was glassy, the wake of a single coot rippling in long lines undisturbed. Walking past the Italian fountains, which were not running yet, Sarah felt that sounds, too, were attenuated. Somewhere in the distance she heard the noise of construction, and she walked carefully, listening to her shoes on the path.

The day before, the squirrels had finally taken a few peanuts from their hands, hers and Amelia's. It had delighted them both and relieved Sarah, as she felt that this was something Amelia would certainly take home with her, something she would remember always about their trip to London. It was worth the time spent, Sarah knew, because Amelia loved animals and would tell all her friends how they'd gone to the Serpentine every morning, persevering until they'd earned the squirrels' trust. It was something they had succeeded in together, and she thought it would grow, over time, into a fond memory for Amelia, an example of her mother at her best.

They were back this morning because Mark wanted to memorialize the event in pictures, a suggestion Sarah appreciated. The squirrels came to their fingertips again, and although it was impossible to tell, she thought they must be the same ones.

"Why don't we name them?" she said to Amelia.

"Name them?"

"Well, after this week, don't you feel like you know them?"

"After this week—" Amelia started, but she stopped and shook her head.

Sarah said cheerfully, "Well, I do. What about George and Lucy? And the one in front of you could be Camilla. Or maybe that's too fancy for a squirrel?"

Amelia remained quiet, avoiding her mother's gaze. A few minutes passed, and Sarah said softly, "I was trying to be funny."

When they had only a handful of peanuts left, Mark came over and said he wanted to give it a try.

Sarah stood. "Why?"

Mark stared at her. "Oh, look. The thing's done. I just want to see if they'll come to me, too. We leave tomorrow."

Amelia, still on the ground, made a stream of kissing noises to soothe the squirrels.

Mark reached for the bag of peanuts Sarah held. When she did not offer it to him, he stuck his hand in awkwardly and took a few. Then he leaned over from the waist, the camera bag swinging forward suddenly. The squirrels scattered.

Sarah said, "It takes patience, Mark. You have to crouch down."

He crouched, and with Amelia clucking and ticking, the squirrels cautiously approached.

"Hold it out to them," Sarah said.

Mark extended his arm.

"It would be better if you put a few on the ground first, until they're used to you."

Amelia looked up. "Mom," she said.

Sarah turned and walked up the path to the clearing. Across the water smoke rose behind Peter Pan and the smell of burning leaves filled the air. With his arms up the way they were— as though conducting a fairy symphony—and the smoke behind him, it looked to Sarah like he was about to jump into the water to escape the fire. She concentrated on him and imagined his dive, just how it would look, how the water would splash up behind his tiny heels and the birds all around would rise and circle in the air, the seagulls' cries echoing over the park. After a while, they would settle down again, unperturbed by the empty pedestal.

When she looked back at Mark and Amelia, they were standing, deep in conversation. The squirrels were gone.

"So," she said, approaching. "I see you two have moved on to more important things."

Mark looked away and Amelia said, "Why are you being like this?"

Sarah was surprised at her answer. "Ask your father," she said and turned to walk alone down the path.

———

She was still in the front yard when Amelia came home. She was on her second rake, the first's handle having splintered. Even in her state, she recognized the agony on Amelia's face, her usual protective distance uprooted by fear and confusion.

Sarah stopped. She wanted to help her. "Amelia," she said. "It's okay."

"Right, Mom. That's great. Will you come inside now?"

"I'm just finishing here."

"Mom, you're done. What are you doing?" Her eyes were red, filling with tears. The bushes on either side of the front door were smashed in sections, holes where thick needles had been. Many of the smaller branches hung down, broken, showing splinters of pulpy white underbark. Trails of leaves ornamented the yard, some of them leading across the driveway and onto the neighbors' grass.

"Oh, sweetie," Sarah started. She took a step toward her, but Amelia took a step back. Sarah dropped the rake.

She leaned over to pick it up, reaching out to balance herself on the ground. "The leaves were, you know, stuck and—"

"Okay, please come inside, Mom. You can tell me there." The tears had been quelled. She was angry now.

"Amelia, you're overreacting. If you'd just listen—"

"Listen? To what? You're hitting the bushes with a rake; the yard is a mess. Were you trying to rake the leaves into the gutter? Because if you were, Mom, you missed. The Mallons aren't going to be very happy."

"Don't worry about it, sweetie."

"Don't call me that! I hate it. No one calls me that except you."

"I'm sorry," Sarah answered. Now that she was no longer raking, she was cold. She didn't have on a coat. Amelia, perhaps sensing that danger was past, turned violently and went into the house. Sarah followed.

When Amelia ran upstairs, Sarah poured herself another drink. She sipped it standing by the kitchen sink and listened to Amelia getting ready to practice. She was upset, she knew, because it wasn't like her to practice first. She usually rested or did some homework. She started with scales and they were fierce and fast. Sarah had played the violin as a child so knew enough to marvel at her daughter's technical ability. She really was so good, Sarah thought. Suddenly she was sad and proud and filled with the desire to tell Amelia that her teacher had said she was good enough to have a concert career. She went upstairs.

The door was closed but unlocked and Sarah opened it without knocking. Amelia ignored her. There was a wicker chair in the corner of the room, and Sarah aimed for it and sat down as quietly as she could. When the chair creaked loudly, she grinned. "Sorry," she whispered.

Amelia finished her scales and warm-up exercises and started thumbing through a book of music. It was clear she wanted Sarah to leave.

"Could I just stay a little bit longer? I really like to listen to you. You're so good."

Amelia looked at her. "Mom, don't do this."

"Do what?"

"Mom, stop."

"Sweet—" she clapped a hand over her mouth. "I don't understand," she said through her fingers.

Amelia glanced around her room as though searching for assistance, then looked down at her violin. "Will you just go away, please?"

"Why? I promise to be quiet. You won't even know I'm here."

"Oh, right. I can smell you."

This was new territory and it surprised them both. Generally they stayed away from the particulars. Amelia stared, waiting, Sarah knew, to see if she would be angry. But she wasn't. It was okay, she thought.

"Yes," she said, swallowing hard. "I know it. But can I tell you why I think I had a drink tonight?"

"No, it's okay," Amelia said quickly. Then they were both quiet and ashamed. The gray light through the blue curtains filled the room. Amelia moved slightly and turned on her music lamp. After a moment, she picked up her violin. She began a slow piece by Satie that Sarah had always loved. It was not something new. It was a piece she'd already performed. A reprieve, Sarah knew, and started to cry, not for the music, but for the time when Amelia would no longer be willing to give her such gifts.

How to Become a Publicist

IN THE MIDWESTERN TOWN where I grew up, my father is repainting my room blue and white, my favorite colors, just in case I come home. I try not to think about this. Instead I concentrate on getting a job as an editorial assistant, not knowing of any other work for a young graduate to do in publishing in New York.

In my first interview, I'm asked to name a few of my favorite authors. This is difficult, I say, blushing—like naming my favorite book. The editor, a woman in her fifties with a bob that comes to two perfect blond points in the hollows of her cheeks, does not smile. When she started in publishing, editorial assistants were essentially secretaries, and she has no sympathy for me. I concentrate and frown gently, trying hard to appear intelligent and serious. Then I name Austen, Dickens, George Eliot, and Hardy, in that order. My concentration was Victorian literature. I haven't read a book shorter than four hundred pages in four years. The editor raises her eyebrows, two perfect arches a shade darker than her hair. I add that I love to read.

My father phones to tell me the room is coming along. He's decided to put up molding and replace the windows. He's doing it himself at night, after work. I tell him the interviews are going well; it shouldn't be much longer now before I'm offered a job.

He says he'll find Mom. I can hear him walking away from the phone, then the faint chimes of their living-room clock. When he comes back, he says that Mom is sleeping. She sleeps a lot these days, he says.

In the next interview, I try different authors. Woolf, Stegner, Hemingway, Joyce Carol Oates? Steinbeck, Faulkner, DeLillo, Alice Munro? I consider adding poets. I'm beginning to wonder if getting a job as an editorial assistant is a matter of matching the right list with the right editor, like a key to a lock. I'm worried that my lists lack artistic integrity, but I've read and enjoyed at least one book by each of these writers. This is the best I can do.

I'm running out of time and money. My roommates-to-be are on an extended postgraduation European tour; I'm living with an aunt and uncle in New Jersey. I'm supposed to have a job by the time they get back. The summer is hot; the city smells of urine. To lift my spirits, my aunt and uncle take me out for Brazilian food. I enjoy the fried bananas, but when the waiter appears with a sword piercing twelve roasted chicken livers, I lose my appetite completely.

———

Eventually I have an interview in my needing-to-be-dry-cleaned interview suit in which I explain that I read a lot of books by a lot of authors. That, strangely, I don't always know who my favorite ones are at any given time. That, instead (and here my voice catches), I feel compelled to read anything anyone recommends. In short, I'm a voracious reader rather than a picky one. I smile desperately. The editor asks if I've considered publicity. I haven't, but her tone is encouraging, so I smile again and say I certainly would. She bows her head and scoots back her chair. She walks me down a long hallway. I can hear energetic, happy voices even before we turn the corner. The exuberance of the place is overwhelming, so different from the quiet editorial offices I've been visiting. In fact, the place is a carnival compared to those morose libraries. This is where I belong!

The editor leaves, and I have an interview with the head of the department, the director of publicity, a woman in her thirties. She is dressed impeccably but has hair that looks real. This seems encouraging. She tells me that publicity is the last stage of bringing a book into the world. It involves care, attention to detail, and above all enthusiasm. Enthusiasm!

"Enthusiasm is contagious," she beams.

Then, seriously, a whisper creeping into her voice, "It's a bit like being a midwife." (Later I will understand that these are pitches. If one angle doesn't work, quickly try another. Adjust tone and volume.)

Publicity reaches out to readers through the medium of the media, she explains.

"Medium of the media," I repeat.

Marketing, she continues, cares more about sales. Publicity worries about the bigger picture, a book's place in the world. But if a publicist does her job well, the result is increased sales. Everything's interrelated!

I smile with enthusiasm.

———————

I tell my dad I have news and ask if Mom is home. He says she is always home. In fact, she rarely leaves the house.

"Great!" I say. "Could you both get on the phone?"

With both of them on the line—my dad in the kitchen, my mom in the family room—I announce that I have a job. My mom is thrilled. She hollers and whoops and says that she knew I could do it, that it's in my blood. All the women on her side of the family have felt this draw to New York. They've gone, worked, burned out, and eventually left. I hear the television on in the background.

"Mom," I say. "Grandma was an alcoholic and Aunt Susan was a dancer. That's a little different."

"Oh, of course it is," she says. "I'm so proud of you."

My father is, too. He's going to keep working on that room, though, because it's far enough along that it should be finished.

My friends return. They have been traveling for two months and still have two weeks before their jobs start. With their mothers, they delve into apartment hunting full-time. I race to meet them during lunch and after work, arriving damp and rumpled, exactly like a piece of wilted lettuce. I dab discreetly at the sweat beading on my upper lip. They smile sadly at me. "You're working so hard," they say.

They want to live on the Upper East Side and have found an apartment building that has everything anyone could want. On the first floor there is a bank, a dry cleaner, and a convenience store. "It's like a little village," one of the mothers says.

"But we're in the middle of New York," I point out.

"Exactly," she says. "This is safer."

In the apartment in the little village, there are two bedrooms. A third, mine, will be created by building a wall in the living room. It will be exactly like living in a closet, only more expensive.

That night we go out to dinner to celebrate the new apartment. I drink too much wine, eat too little food. When they start telling me how much they admire me for moving to New York all alone, I tell them it's just part of my family history, actually. All the women on my mother's side have come to New York, lived, burned out, and eventually left. They stare at me while I laugh. Sinatra starts "New York, New York" over the restaurant speakers, and I excuse myself from the table. Unfortunately, the music is piped into the bathroom as well.

———————

At work, I'm learning to write press releases. At first these seem like short essays about a book in which only positive things are said. My first attempt is for a biography of Shakespeare by an eminent scholar. I begin: *William Shakespeare's contemporary Ben Jonson wrote, "He was not of an age but for all time." These words were written soon after Shakespeare's death, when it had yet to be proven whether his plays would indeed last for all time.* I work on the press release at night, after work.

The release is rejected. The publicity director tells me, in between phone calls, that it sounds too much like an essay. "You're writing for book reviewers," she says, covering the mouthpiece with her palm. "And radio and television producers. These people don't have a lot of time. They want to read the release, get a sense of the book, make a quick decision and go on."

This reminds me, I say, of Raymond Carver's advice about writing short stories, "Get in, get out, go on."

"Exactly," she says, to me or the phone, I'm not sure which.

I try again. *In SHAKESPEARE: A LIFE, the author studies the playwright's triumph over the vicissitudes of time.*

"Forget you were an English major," she says.

Who was Shakespeare? In this breakthrough study, the mystery is revealed.

"Good," she says. Five hundred copies are printed and distributed to editors and producers around the country. It's thrilling, almost like being published.

I cannot live with the two friends on the Upper East Side. They have Laura Ashley quilts and intend to buy Laura Ashley curtains. They tell me the beat-up dresser I got for fifty dollars at a church sale in Chelsea is quaint. I tell them it's solid maple, and I love it. When I pull out, they are frustrated; they will have to get a smaller apartment. I promise to keep in touch, kiss them on the cheeks. In a year I will not remember their last names.

I find a barely affordable studio at Ninety-ninth and Broadway. The kitchen sink is five steps from my bed, and feathers float around the bathroom from the pigeons roosting on the windowsill. There is a brick wall not three feet from both of the windows. The dresser, however, looks great, and my mother tells me to be happy I have a window in the bathroom at all. They're rare, she says, starting to cry.

"Mom!" I say. "Both of our bathrooms have windows!"

She says, "In New York, I mean. In New York."

I say, "Mom, do you need me to come home? I can come home, Mom."

She says, "Don't be silly. Your life's there now."

I begin to settle in. Someone points out that the first letters of the avenues west from Central Park West spell CAB. This is surprisingly helpful. I learn that to get to Central Park I should walk down Broadway to at least Ninety-sixth Street before turning east. This way I avoid a pocket of drug dealers and other shady characters. I can, however, walk straight over to Riverside Drive on Ninety-ninth; that neighborhood is wealthy and safe. I find a good dry cleaner.

Soon there are things I love: the lanes of unscathed sky between the skyscrapers in Midtown; the Chrysler Building on cloudy days; the sunset reflected in the building across the street from my office; the undulating expanse of Central Park, like actors offstage waving a giant green sheet in the middle of the city: Voilà! A park! I don't go below Midtown much; the chaotic streets at the bottom of the island are a challenge I'm not ready to face. I love the orderliness of the blocks on the Upper West Side and hope that does not make me a certain kind of New Yorker, although it probably does. Everything in New York seems like a potential label. I bought a new pair of leather shoes, and the first time I wore them to work someone said, "Very Upper West Side."

Occasionally I see things that upset me, such as the man who kicked out at a passing car's tire, apparently for no other reason than that the car was rushing through a yellow light. The force of the kick pulled him off the curb, and jerked his extremely pregnant wife into the gutter with him.

Sometimes I look at the ground, covered as far as the eye can see in cement, and feel something akin to panic. Where does the real ground begin? What, exactly, is New York resting on? I try to look up, although I've been told only tourists do that.

The publicity director asks me to work on a few of my own books. As the newest member of the department, however, I get the books no one else wants: a dictionary of women composers, a treatise on the building and preserving of American schooners, a book of photographs of the coast of Oregon, and a history of the zipper called *Zipper!* For the schooner book, I throw a publication party at the South Street Seaport. For *Zipper!* I send out the publicity materials in little zippered pouches. These ideas are big hits, and I am promoted.

The leaves begin to change, even the fifteen or so on the maple sapling in front of my apartment building. Walking to work with a cup of hot coffee and a fresh bran muffin, I have moments of happiness. I'm having trouble making my school loan payments and have started charging my groceries, but on these cold mornings, with my steaming coffee and my muffin, everything seems possible.

The publicity director says I'm especially presentable. When she is busy, she often asks me to escort her authors to events in the city. On one such occasion I sit in the studio audience of a popular late-night talk show. When the host comes out, he talks to the audience for a while. He makes a joke of the fact that I'm sitting in his audience with a book on my lap. He pretends to be insulted. I try to explain why I have the book, that the author is going to be one of his guests, but I'm not miked and no one can hear me. Everyone laughs. Later, when I tell the publicity director what happened, she says I should have held the book up in front of my face. "Think like a publicist," she says.

At parties, men want to give me their manuscripts. They whisper plot summaries in my ear. They'd rather be talking to an editorial assistant, but I am second best, way above the assistants in subsidiary rights. I drop the manuscripts in the slush pile first thing Monday morning. I'm starting to believe that this is thinking like a publicist.

At Christmastime, I call my mom from Rockefeller Plaza. I think it will make her happy to know I can see the tree, but she starts to cry. There's no place in the world like New York at Christmas, she says. Her voice sounds small and choked.

A fabulously beautiful woman is waiting to use the phone. Her long winter coat looks like cashmere, and her hands are cozily tucked into a white fur muff. She looks Russian, as if she'd just dismounted from a sleigh. I turn toward the phone box and hunch over the receiver.

"I miss New York," my mom is saying. "Why did I leave?" She seems to be asking me, but I know that she's just thinking out loud. I've heard this before.

"Oh, right. To marry your father." Her voice is small and hard.

I peek out at the waiting lady. A well-dressed man is talking to her, offering her the use of his cell phone. He saw her waiting; he gestures at me in the booth and shivers to indicate how cold it is. This is what happens, it seems, when you are beautiful. The world just provides assistance.

I ask my mom if she's ever thought about volunteering, perhaps with children or animals? Maybe she would find this fulfilling?

There's a long pause, during which I can hear her sniffling. Then she asks if I can see the skaters. Yes, I say. I can see the skaters.

She blows her nose. She is so proud of me.

I ask about my brother.

He leaves for college next year!

The following week, I attend the Christmas party in the lobby of my apartment building: twelve people standing around with wine in plastic cups and store-bought Christmas cookies. A tree has appeared in the corner, shackled in heavy yellow garland. Next to it a grim plastic reindeer wades through deep drifts of sticky-looking cotton. There's a bad dent above his right eye. A woman in a Christmas sweater greets me. She's responsible for the party and clearly the epicenter of cheer.

You're in time for the carols, she says, handing me a cup of wine and a clutch of cookies on a red napkin. Just then a woman begins "O Holy Night." Her voice is beautiful; everyone is taken aback and no one wants to join in. People motion for her to continue alone, and she smiles through the words, tipping her head in a little bow of acknowledgment. Someone near me whispers that she is an opera singer, she's in the chorus at the Met. Others nod in agreement. The fluorescent lights seem to soften, the tree stands taller under its load of garland, and this, I think, is the promise of New York. Here, in this dingy lobby, in this no-man's-land above the fashionable section of the Upper West Side, is an angel, a singer of true talent. Her voice, reverberating majestically in the little lobby of this warm, smelly building, reminds me why I came to New York. My eyes fill with tears. I start to sniffle and have to dump my cookies to blow my nose.

For Christmas, I give everyone in my family books from the publishing house. I've read none of them and wrap quickly. When I'm home, all the friends and neighbors who have heard that I work in publishing think I'm an editor. Explaining to each of them what a publicist does is tiring. After a few glasses of wine, however, it gets easier. It's a lot like being a cheerleader, I say.

———

In the spring, I'm promoted to full publicist. I work on a book called *Wistful Moors*, a first novel based on the life of Charlotte Brontë. It's my first big project; rather than the midlist dregs I've been working on, this is a novel with "breakout potential" according to the publishing executives at my house. It's a novel with "legs," they say.

"Oh, yeah," says the publicity director in the weekly publicity meeting. "It's a book that might just get up and walk itself to the bestseller list. What do they think we *do* around here?"

"Hello. You've reached the producers of the D— R— show. Please leave a message after the beep. If you are a *publicist* calling about an author interview, please leave a *brief* message. We receive an enormous number of calls from publicists daily, and it is simply impossible for us to respond to all of you. Howeverwedothankyouforyourideas." Beep.

"I'm calling about *Wistful Moors*—"

"This mailbox is full."

"Hi, I'm a publicist for—"

"Fax the information."

"I'm calling to follow up—"

"Which book."

"*Wistful Moors.* It's a novel about the life of Charlotte Brontë. Do you know—"

"Just fax the information."

"Can you tell me if the book has arrived?"

"Unlikely. We get hundreds every day."

On a Sunday night in May, I call home. My voice is hoarse
from a week of intense phone pitching for *Wistful Moors*. My
mother asks if I'm sick. I laugh wildly for a moment, then clear
my throat. "No," I say. "I'm fine. How are you?"

"Oh, fine, fine," she says.

I ask if she liked her Mother's Day present, a book of essays
by daughters about their mothers.

"I do. I do. Is it a book you're working on?" she asks.

It is, when I can get away from *Wistful Moors*. I realize with a
start that I forgot a card and sent the book with a press release
wrapped around it.

The author of *Wistful Moors* goes on a short reading tour. One
night she reads at one of the best independent bookstores in the
Midwest, a shop that has been around for decades. That night,
around the corner, the popular author of a new legal thriller
reads at a brand-new Barnes & Noble. There are two hundred
people at Barnes & Noble, five at the *Wistful Moors* reading. The
next morning, the author calls me in tears.

I take a deep breath and tell her that those five people who
heard her last night will tell friends about the book, that she
should never underestimate the power of word of mouth, that
the bookstore where she read is a really good one, that they'll
prominently display the book and continue to hand sell it for
weeks, that this is more significant in the long run than the 30
percent discount on the other book at Barnes & Noble, that a lot
of good will come out of last night even if it doesn't feel like it.

While I'm speaking, my left eyelid begins to twitch.

I start collecting essays by authors complaining about their book tours. The form has become, in fact, a new genre—the obligatory just-returned-from-book-tour essay about the trials and tribulations of traveling around the country. Partly these are boastful. After all, the publisher has deemed the author worthy of the expense of a tour. And partly they are self-important—the author prefers, *needs*, to be at home, *writing*. Completing the script are nostalgia for the historical role of the writer, anger at the stupidity of the media, frustration with the youth and inexperience of the average publicist, and stories of humiliation at being made to get up at ungodly hours for interviews with hosts who haven't read their books.

At the weekly publicity meeting, I show the department my collection. I ask if they've noted this irony: at first it was only the big authors who were sent on tour, and now it is only the big authors who are allowed to refuse to go. Furthermore, all of them, big and small, like to complain about it. So why are we sending them? I ask. Around the room there are tight-lipped smiles, a few shrugs. Authors are just notoriously difficult, the publicity director says.

A few weeks later, at a major book-award ceremony, the fiction winner, an esteemed novelist, uses her acceptance speech to relate stories about all the screwups and fiascoes of her book tour. The audience, mostly editors and other writers, laughs heartily. I cut a picture of this writer out of a magazine, draw a mustache on it, and tape it to my door. The next day the director calls me into her office. She's worried about me, she says. And she wants to talk about *Wistful Moors*. It seems the editor is frustrated with the amount of publicity the book has received and wants us to try the big league, the TV talk shows. The publicity director admits our chances with a first novel of this kind are next to nothing, but the effort will get the editor off her back.

I practice my pitch out loud before the first call. To my astonishment, I get through the line of assistants but am brought to a halt by the first producer.

"Why would we be interested in a book by Emily Brontë?"

"Well, she's always been such a perennial favorite, Charlotte Brontë. Emily, too, of course, but this novel is about *Charlotte* Brontë, the author of *Jane Eyre?* The author grew up in Nebraska and from a young age identified with the Brontë sisters. She was moved by the parallels between the English moors and the Great Plains. This is her first novel, and we think it has breakout potential."

"Okay, well, we'll take a look at it."

I press on. "Many women, you know, grow up loving the Brontë books, and now they could read a novel about Charlotte. It's already appealing to women's book groups around the country. Did you know her brother and two sisters died within nine months of each other?"

"The author's?"

"No, Charlotte's. She nursed them all. She withstood so much loneliness and stress—"

"The author?"

"No, Charlotte, but still managed to be a successful writer. Many of her concerns were very modern."

"Right."

"Do you know if the book has arrived?"

"No."

"No, you don't know, or no—"

"I don't think it's here."

"I'd be happy to send another copy."

"Fine."

When I hang up, I cry "Medic!" exactly like a wounded soldier on the battlefield, but not loud enough for anyone to actually hear.

On a hot summer night, the city again smelling of urine, I drink too much with an Irish author in New York on book tour. All publicists, at one time or another, drink too much with an Irish author in New York on book tour. Trying to pay the bill, I'm told that the place doesn't take credit cards. This confuses me. "But how will we pay?" I ask. Everyone at the table laughs. "Remember cash?" someone says. The Irish author says this is wonderful; he's going to use it in his next book.

I start to see the word "publicity" associated with very negative things. The NRA, for example. I read somewhere that publicity has been called "the black art." It is always vaguely responsible for the deaths of movie stars.

The thought that I promote books is some consolation. Books are good. But deep down I'm beginning to feel like a salesman. I rent *Death of a Salesman*, with Dustin Hoffman, and watch it alone over my eighth consecutive dinner of ramen noodles. After the movie, staring at the moonlight on the bricks outside my window, I try to think of all the words that can be spelled with the letters of publicity. I'm stuck on *pubic* when I fall asleep on the sofa.

Promotional words begin to annoy me, especially: *luminous, stunning, mesmerizing. Colossal, odyssey, tour de force. Ambitious, exhilarating, heartbreaking, breathtaking* (in fact, all words with *heart* or *breath* in them). The worst is when they appear together in press releases and jacket copy. *Luminously mesmerizing,* for example.

I reconsider graduate school, buy study books for the GRE, and spend one whole Saturday in the Barnes & Noble at Eighty-second Street writing away for application materials.

In the meantime, I decide I have to do something besides publicity, so I sign up for a creative writing workshop. Taking the 6 to Astor Place after work on Tuesday nights makes me feel edgy, sensitive, hyper-aware. A woman sitting across from me on the subway begins to yawn, her fat chin breaking into a constellation of dimples. "Constellation of dimples," I write down in the notebook I've started keeping in my purse. I'm drinking a lot of coffee. My hands tremble, but I feel good, strong. I write a story about a mother and a daughter in which the daughter feels enormous guilt and pressure because she is the focus of the mother's life. The class is not enthusiastic. One woman, who has said previously that her mother died when she was ten, and who writes stories about young girls enjoying scrumptious food-filled summers in the German Alps, glares fiercely at me across the table. She thinks my story is unrealistic.

I write another about a publicist who one day, after her millionth phone call to a curt producer, decides to become the Unabomber of the media world. Radio and television producers all over the country die, and a great reformation begins in which publicists are the supreme arbiters of literary taste and style. The class doesn't like this one either. Someone says I use too many adjectives.

The motherless woman continues to scowl at me, even when it isn't my story being read.

At this point, one of three things could happen. Waiting for the graduate school materials to arrive, my irony will slowly fade and I'll start to say things like, "Her style is sort of Willa Cather meets Cormac McCarthy" without cringing. If this happens, I'll go on to be a great publicist, maybe a publicity director someday, or the head of my own agency. I'll meet my two friends running in Central Park one weekend and I'll greet them with *enthusiasm*, suggest coffee, and over steaming cappuccinos use my best conspiratorial whisper to tell them stories about all the famous writers I've worked with. They will ask about my mother, and although she has suffered what the doctors are calling a "nervous breakdown," I'll describe her as a victim of the "empty nest syndrome." A pitch. Easier to explain.

Alternatively, my eye twitch will worsen, and I'll start to gesture wildly during phone pitches, like a drowning woman clutching at air. At publication parties, I'll forget to talk about the book being feted and the grand media plans I have for it. Instead, I'll share my theories. I'll ask people if they've noticed that often a writer's entire career can be traced in his or her flap copy. They will shake their heads and stare blankly. Do they remember, I'll try again, books from the library when they were little? Books without jackets, without flap copy, just the naked book with its library binding? Silence. I'll grow breathless, overheated. We live in an age of author molds, I'll insist. Don't you see? We force authors through right-shaped holes, just like a child's shape-sorter! People will move slowly away from me.

But it is the third possibility that frightens me the most. I'm beginning to dream about returning to the blue-and-white room. My parents know nothing about this. When they call, I tell them I love New York and am doing just fine.

Refuge

O<small>N A FRIDAY MORNING</small> in May, the brand-new
maroon-and-gold lobby of Potomac Run was
filled with a sea of blue-and-white L.L. Bean bags. They were
large bags, the kind to take on a day sail or to the beach. All had
been monogrammed G&G for Garraty and Grimes, the
esteemed Washington law firm, and the stiff nautical canvas of
privilege and good health was filling the lobby with a heady fragrance. Potomac Run, a secluded hotel in rural Virginia's business corridor, was an hour's drive from Washington, D.C., and
fifteen minutes from Dulles International Airport. It was surrounded by a golf course, a man-made lake, and, here and there,
the remains of the forest subdued into geometrical shapes, a
triangle, a parallelogram. To the north, an assisted-living facility hid in a man-made dell. To the south, several nascent software companies operated quietly in buildings that looked like
glass cubes.

To Shelley Dixon, arriving for the G&G weekend retreat with
a small black bag she had always used for the beach, Potomac
Run was clearly trying to emulate the historic spas of the Virginia mountains, such as the Homestead, and doing it poorly.
There was the same central tower flanked by two wings, but it
was built of red bricks that were new and unweathered and

seemed too smooth. It was also missing the front porch lined with rocking chairs where, at the Homestead, people would have been sipping lemonade.

Shelley came through the central glass doors and stopped abruptly. She'd once seen an art installation in the cloister of a cathedral, thousands of miniature terra-cotta human figures filling the flagstone space. The repetitiveness of it had mesmerized her just as the blue-and-white bags, in their stiff slouchy postures, did now. She saw in each bag the bill of a baseball cap, the shine of a windbreaker, the neck of a wine bottle. There was almost certainly a box of golf balls at the bottom, probably a mousepad. Everything, she knew, would be monogrammed. The bounty of corporate retreat.

She stared at the bags until she was aware that she'd been standing still longer than was acceptable, or at least easily explainable. She sidestepped out of the way of a porter but still couldn't will her body to move toward the reception tables set up in the lobby's corner. Two mornings earlier her fifteen-year-old son, Jason, had left for Seattle with his father. Not, as Jason thought before his father arrived, just for the summer, but permanently. Over the past two years, she'd watched him become depressed and disobedient. He had started skipping school and ignoring Shelley, her advice, her pleading. She could no longer help or handle him, she thought, and worried that the longer she tried, the greater the chance she would lose him altogether. When his father arrived, they had surprised Jason with the plan.

When she made it to the tables to check in, two bags were pushed toward her. "Is it two per person?" she asked, turning the neck of one of the wine bottles to see the label.

The woman behind the table, one of the secretaries, marked

something on her clipboard and handed Shelley a name tag.
"The wine? One per bag."

"No, the bags," said Shelley.

"Two per room."

"That's ridiculous. I'm alone."

"All right." The secretary lifted one of the bags off the table
and placed it behind her, out of commission.

"But I'll tell you what," Shelley said. "Why don't you let me
have the bottle from the second bag and we'll call it even."

The secretary looked up, unsure of the answer to this
unprecedented request.

"Oh, come on," Shelley said. "We work for the same company. There's no reason to be so regimented." She leaned over,
pulled out the wine, and wedged it down into the first bag.
"There," she said. "Thank you."

Shelley was forty-seven and a fourth-year associate at G&G
for the second time. This made her something of a conundrum
for the staff and attorneys alike. No one knew exactly how to
treat her or what to say when she cavalierly summed up her
irregular history, as she often did over a drink. Twenty years ago
she'd left G&G, she'd say, despite promises that she was a good
candidate for partnership. "Candidate for partnership," she'd
repeat with a smile, remembering the words as they were spoken to her then. "Isn't that great?" The partners didn't speak
that way anymore. Now you were or were not "partner material." She went to graduate school, earned a master's degree, and
left a dissertation on Henry James unfinished. She married,
moved to England, gave birth to Jason. Eventually she finished
the dissertation, and when they moved back to America, she
taught English at a small liberal arts college in the East for a
while. Then David left her and she needed a better-paying job,

she'd say simply, raising her eyebrows over her whiskey and water.

"Is this woman causing problems?"

Shelley turned to see Dick Latimer, a senior G&G tax partner. "Just making sure I get my full retreat benefits," she said.

Shelley was not a casually affectionate person, but when she did hug someone, as she did Latimer now, she squeezed hard. Latimer's soft round stomach warmed against her own. He'd interviewed her when she first came to the firm and had been instrumental in getting the partnership to let her come back.

"How are you doing?" he asked. His voice had an unusual cadence, full and slow. It was one of the things Shelley liked about him. He never used the abbreviation for the Internal Revenue Service but always scrupulously pronounced each word.

"Well, considering Jason left on Wednesday and I have to spend the whole weekend here, not too bad."

Latimer watched her. "It's not your fault," he said.

"He was less surprised than I thought he'd be," she confessed, a detail she hadn't meant to share with anyone. She straightened and smiled. "I don't suppose you could get me a second chance at *that* job?"

She flung her old bag over her shoulder and picked up her new one. She bounced past the superfluous ground-floor amenities of Potomac Run, a fire in balmy weather, snack mix in the morning. She saw two other sets of hospitality bags—one gold with a piece of white tissue paper decoratively sticking out the top, the other green with fresh oranges and bottles of mineral water—and wondered how many corporate retreats Potomac Run could contain at one time. Strangely, the third-floor hallway smelled of birdseed, she thought, and her room had the scent of laundered sheets and dusty curtains, with a hint of caulk mixed in from the bathroom. She looked for the minibar, planning to chill her wine, but there wasn't one. The room was spacious but ordinary: an exasperating king-size bed, a large entertainment center, a table by the window with two chairs. Disappointed, she walked down the hall and filled a bucket with ice. When she returned, she left the bucket on the table and stood by the windows. The heavy floral curtains were tied back, leaving the gauzy white privacy curtain. It reminded her of English tearooms boxed in by lace, that desire to see but not be seen. She had a view of the golf course, the edge of the forest where the decimation had halted, and one bald hill, a lonely bump on the horizon, obviously man-made.

Friday afternoons at Potomac Run were filled with obligatory, half-hour business meetings in rooms with names like Sycamore, Oak, and Redbud. All the conference rooms were named for trees and flowers in what felt like a late and meager attempt to camouflage the damage done. After the meetings, the attendees were released to leisure. Golf carts buzzed around the circular drive between the pro shop and the first green. The spa filled with spouses. Some people lingered over lunch in the Grill Room, others retired to their rooms for a nap. By five o'clock, the name tags reappeared and everyone roamed the hallways carrying drinks. The scene had all the dissolution of Bourbon Street, Shelley thought, with none of the joie de vivre.

She'd found her way to the G&G Hospitality Suite, the Magnolia Room, and was drinking with Mike Haskett, one of the senior tax partners. Short and stocky, his mass seemingly centered in his neck and shoulders, he reminded Shelley of a cartoon rocket that bunched at the front before blasting off. But he was going through a divorce and smiled as little as she did, which she liked. Both of them were deliberately not commenting on how many large glasses of wine the other took from the hospitality supply.

People began to wander in with fresh sunburns and the smell of wind on their clothes. The sun was setting out the window but at a bad angle, the light blinding on the smudged glass. Tim Huggins, a star sixth-year associate, came in shielding his eyes in what looked like a salute. "Socializing with associates, I see, Mike. Better pace yourself."

The contradiction between Shelley's age and her status often reduced people to teasing her in third person. Stage-whisper gossip was common.

Mike dropped his newspaper and squinted into the sun. The effect was menacing. "Shelley's just been telling me the secret of eternal youth."

"Yes, plenty of wine and no exercise. Too bad for you, Tim," she said, looking at his golf shoes and muscular arms.

"I plan to catch up. At least on the wine."

"Good luck," Mike said. "We've been here a while, Shelley longer than I."

She wondered if he meant the Magnolia Room or G&G. Both were true. She'd left the firm the year before he started.

"Well, I wouldn't have been if I could have chilled the wine they gave us. What exactly are you supposed to do with warm Virginia white wine?"

"Age it?" Tim suggested.

Dinner that evening was a barbecue on the back terrace. When Shelley arrived, she surveyed the scene, then skirted the perimeter and went straight to the bar. "Look at me," she said to the bartender, plucking at her blue shirt and black pants. "I'm a walking bruise. I didn't realize a sundress was required." She ordered a whiskey and water and learned the bartender's name was Martin. Something about his jaw when he smiled reminded her of Jason.

"How old are you?" she asked.

"Twenty-eight."

"I guarantee this won't be a fun night. They're all lawyers. You'll probably get home early."

He smiled. "So I better not spill anything, you're saying, or I might get sued?"

"Exactly." Across the terrace someone started tapping a glass for a toast. "Let me have another one," Shelley said, holding up her drink. "Who knows when I'll be able to get back."

The retreat was intended to celebrate the recent acquisition of a small New York law firm, giving G&G the New York office it had long desired, and one of the New York partners, hedgy about being invited south for a retreat, wanted to give a speech before dinner. He climbed onto a wooden planter and, when he had the group's attention, began gesturing emphatically with a glass of red wine. He wanted to define the uniting of these two great firms, he said, as less of an acquisition and more of a merger. Much more. The wineglass tipped precariously and the people standing beneath him pressed back into the crowd. Washington was calm and genteel, he explained, New York busy and rude. There was laughter and some light booing from the crowd. But with the manners of the former and the work ethic of the latter, he continued confidently, he was sure they'd make a perfect law firm. He raised his glass. "To G&G," he finished, and then, after a cue from one of the staff, "Dinner is served."

The tables had centerpieces featuring hurricane lamps and

candles, but nothing was lit. In the gloaming, it was still just possible to determine texture and shape at the buffet, allowing the lawyers to distinguish between rice and potato salad, chicken wings and ribs. The issue of open seating was creating a stir. Most associates were giddy with the freedom of it and were quickly establishing large partner-free zones. Others were being tapped.

"Brad, sit with us," Shelley heard from one of the real-estate partners.

"Tim. Grab a seat at our table." This was Latimer to Tim Huggins. Shelley looked up. "You come, too," he added. "I think there's room."

When she got there, however, the table was full. She stood for a moment behind Latimer's chair with her plate and her silverware wrapped in heavy linen and stared at the bodies around the table, willing one of them to dissolve. She couldn't hold it against Latimer; it wasn't his job to take care of her. "I think there's room at Mike's table," he said apologetically.

Mike was seated with a mixed group of associates and partners. Shelley recognized Natalia Jones with her husband and new baby. She was the youngest partner, her specialty litigation, yet she had an odd habit of starting her sentences with "Now, I may be wrong about this." She often was, but because she'd started in such a way, people felt an obligation to reassure. She was enormously successful. Seth Cooper was also there, another fourth-year tax associate. Shelley didn't know anyone else and Mike didn't turn to her when she took the seat next to him.

She glanced around the terrace with growing dismay. The tables were full, the convivial sounds of eating and drinking filled the night air, but there was no lighting other than the landscaping illumination embedded under trees. When she asked one of the waiters if he had matches, she received the small smile of full-service. Potomac Run couldn't allow her to light the candles herself; someone would do it for her. The waiter returned ten minutes later with a lighter. With this he burned his fingers lighting the small votive candles and failed altogether with the hurricane lamp. After he'd gone, the candles went out, extinguished by the breath and laughter of the young associates.

"Are these the new austerity measures you were telling us about, Mike?" Seth Cooper, one arm around his wife, picked up a daisy from the spring flowers strewn among the place settings and twirled it in his fingers. "China at a barbecue, but no vases?"

Mike scowled.

"Does anyone have matches?" Shelley asked. A few people shook their heads.

"Doesn't anyone smoke?"

Natalia raised her eyebrows, others at the table shook their heads. Shelley was astonished to realize that her desire to shed light on the dinner—actually, metaphorically—was beginning to outweigh her sense of decorum.

"How many here have done work for our esteemed client Philip Morris?" she asked, and the conversation at the table instantly refracted. "They're from the NBA," Natalia said, turning to the person on her right.

"Who is?"

"I represent them, but I don't defend them," the man next to Shelley said quietly.

She didn't know him. "Philip Morris?"

"The NBA," Natalia was saying. "The tall guys with the gold borders on their name tags."

"Oh, the National Booksellers Association," Shelley said. "Of course."

"Very funny. They're the NBA rookies here for a cultural enrichment program."

"At *Potomac Run?*" Shelley said, then excused herself before she could say anything else, remembering that her tendency to behave this way upset Jason.

"Has it ever occurred to you," he said one night, "to just go to work and do your job without making fun of everything? If you hate the place so much, why don't you leave?"

"It's not that easy," she'd said, sobered by the ferocity of his outburst. She hadn't realized how much her flippancy worried him.

She thought she might have more potato salad, but the buffet was now completely dark. An enterprising young member of the staff had recognized the problem and posted herself by the main courses. "Pork, chicken, beef," she recited in order, over and over, but there was nothing to be done for the salads. Someone deflected a landscaping light at the edge of the building, casting a misty beam across the desserts and illuminating the bar.

Shelley greeted Martin as if he were an old friend, and he poured a whiskey and water without being asked. "Can you explain this darkness?" she asked, gesturing at her event.

He looked at the terrace. "Not my department, but here's a pack of matches. Maybe they'll do some good."

Her cheeks felt numb, which was the first sign she'd had too much to drink, but the darkness of the event was preposterous, historic. She took the matches and drifted toward the tables.

"Spring has sprung," she heard someone say. A man laughed.

"I don't know. I guess I hear Sinatra's voice behind the words and they don't seem so silly."

"Oh, Sheila," said someone at another table. "Thank you. You're a genius."

"Shelley lived in England for a time, didn't you?" This was Andrew Hawthorne, a senior corporate partner and a member of the managing committee. He was an athletic man who liked to say he had a theoretical interest in history—theoretical because he didn't have time to pursue it. He introduced her to one of the corporate associates, Alan Robbins, who had been assigned to the London office six months ago. This was his first trip back.

Shelley perched on an empty seat next to him. "How do you like it?" she asked.

"The office?"

"England."

"Oh, we like it now but it took a while. Two cultures separated by their common language, you know." He smiled and Shelley saw that he had perfect American teeth—straight, white, set tightly together. The English would hold it against him, and Shelley was not sure that she didn't.

"I always thought they had more time," she said. "There just seemed to be more time in England."

He looked thoughtful. "Yes, more time. I know what you mean," but it was clear he did not, and Shelley rose. She loved England. Her happiest years as a mother had been spent there and she would not make platitudes about it with a stranger. "Lovely to meet you," she said in her best English accent and floated away.

"You have what it takes," drifted to her from another table, the alluring and persuasive voice of litigation.

"I'm sorry? What do I have?" the timid reply.

When she had visited all the tables, she stood at the boundary of the event and surveyed her work. Candlelight lapped at the shadows and bounced and gleamed off windows. Shelley

stood in the grass—the rough of the eighteenth hole, she realized—and wiggled her open-toe sandals in the evening dew.
Then she walked back to the bar and Martin handed her
another drink.

"And there was light," he said with a grand sweep of his arm.

She bowed and tried to thank him, but could only shake her
head. Because of his smile, his jaw, she'd imagined Jason speaking and it momentarily stripped her glaze of self-control.

She woke Saturday morning dreaming of reveille. She was on
her stomach, propped up on her elbows, her fists clenched. She
flopped on her back and straightened her arms at her sides. This
was not the first time she'd started the day in such a position. It
had been happening for weeks. Her arms were asleep from her
fingertips to her shoulders, and her elbows, she knew, gently
flexing them, would be stiff for the rest of the day.

The ice bucket had spent the night perspiring and now a
smooth puddle ran over the table and the wine was again warm.
There was a soggy spot on the carpet that smelled of cigarettes
although the room was supposed to be nonsmoking. She'd left
the curtains open, as she always did, so the morning light would
wake her, and she looked sadly at the edge of the forest. She'd
studied a map in the lobby the day before and knew that it was
doomed, lying as it did in Development Areas C and D. A second golf course was planned, another conference center.

When she turned, she saw the message light on the telephone. She hadn't noticed it when she came in the night before,
late, tired, drunk. There'd been a post-dinner party in Tim Huggins's room and she vaguely remembered discussing with a

group of associates the possibility of an excursion to the out-
let mall. It had been her idea, a kind of renegade outing to
escape the retreat, like a bunch of kids ditching summer camp.
It was the sort of thing she might have done to impress Jason.
She was the mom he and his friends liked best because she was
lenient, funny, honest. She told Jason things other parents hid.
This made them close when he was younger, but as he grew he
seemed confused and embarrassed by her confessions, her
largesse. Once she told him about the time his father asked her
on the phone after she'd been in a bike accident whether or not
her face had been hurt. It was his first question. Her face? What
did it matter where she was hurt? She was in the hospital!

"Great, Mom. So Dad's a callous son-of-a-bitch," he'd said,
wilting under the strain of conflicting loyalties. "What am I
supposed to do with that?"

She picked up the phone and covered her eyes with her hand.

"Hi, Mom. It's me. Dad said we should call to say we're all
right and everything." There was a pause. She could hear David's
voice behind him, but not the words.

"Yeah, we're in South Dakota," Jason continued. "The Badlands. Actually, yeah, we took a walk in Badlands National Park
today. It was really cool. We saw a thunderstorm coming. The
sky is so big, I don't know if you've been—Dad says no. Well,
you can see different weather patterns at the same time. It was
sunny where we were but in the distance you could see these
huge black clouds and rain and lightning. It was really cool."
There was another silence.

"Dad says . . . Yeah, right, so I'm okay and I miss you. Dad
says we'll call again soon. Bye, Mom."

She listened to the message three more times. David had
prompted the Badlands story, it was obvious, but at the end she

thought she could detect Jason's own feeling. He'd said he missed her. More important, he had sounded like himself when he said it. That indifferent, monotonous tone she had come to dread was gone. He'd forgotten it or left it behind. But he hadn't sounded worried or upset, either, and she realized that she'd been hoping to hear in his voice some indication that the reality, the severity, of the situation had sunk in. Even if he'd been angry with her. Anything would have been better than the complacency with which he had climbed into his father's car. He couldn't wait to see the Badlands, he'd said.

This isn't a vacation, she'd wanted to scream. You're leaving me, I'm sending you away!

"Did you know the name refers to a geological formation?" he said as he put the last of his boxes in the backseat. He looked up at his father. "I read about them in school."

"No, you didn't. I told you that," Shelley said.

David and Jason stared at her.

She waved her hand in front of her face, flicking away the gnat of her emotion, her maternal love. What good had it done either of them? She moved forward, hugged him, managed to let go. Then she stood on the front stoop methodically waving good-bye until the car had turned the corner at the end of the block.

———

When she came down a little after eight, the fire in the lobby had already been started. Or maybe it was still going, she thought, never extinguished, like the flame in a Jewish temple. The bowls of snack mix had been refreshed and everything was quiet. Potomac Run's ability to absorb large groups of people seemed miraculous. Where were the NBA rookies? Culture or no culture, surely they had to practice. Shelley wished to hear the sound of basketballs in the distance, something hard and real.

She had no appetite for breakfast, so avoided the Sunrise Buffet and entered the maze of carpeted corridors in the North Wing. She peeked into several small conference rooms: Spruce, Sugar Maple, Plum. At the end of the wing, the hallway widened into a small round room. There was a trickling fountain in the center surrounded by platters of muffins and pastries, cereal and granola bars, coffee, tea, and many varieties of soda and sparkling water. A bank of pay phones hung on a wall nearby and one of them started ringing.

Just then Natalia appeared from behind her, dressed in the G&G retreat T-shirt. She looked questioningly at Shelley, then walked over to the phone. "No one there," she said cheerfully, replacing the receiver.

"They told me I'd find mineral water here." Natalia walked over to the table and removed a bottle of Evian. "Are you going running?" she asked.

Shelley looked down at her clothes. She was wearing tennis shoes and an old T-shirt, a loose pair of pants, but she had not intended to run. She shook her head.

"Oh. I thought we could go together." She opened the bottle of water and took a sip. "How are you, Shelley?" she said, wiping the wet from her upper lip. "You don't seem yourself."

Shelley wondered what she could mean. They didn't know each other well. There was a decade between them, but it might as well have been a century. She felt as if she'd raised her baby in a different age. Natalia was frequently offered as a model to young women joining G&G straight out of law school who had lifestyle concerns. *See,* her example was meant to say, *You can make partner and start a family at the same time.* Shelley's life had been more linear.

She walked to the table and picked up a box of juice. "Is your baby a girl or a boy?" she asked.

"A boy," Natalia said. "Edward."

"How old is he?"

"Five months. Do you have children?"

"Yes. A boy."

"How old?"

"Fifteen."

"Oh, a hard age."

Shelley nodded.

"Well, I may be wrong about this, but you look like you could use a real vacation, not this place. The spa's nice, though. Have you been?"

"I wasn't going to."

"All the appointments are taken, but why don't you take mine? I've got a facial at two-thirty, but I don't need it. I had a massage yesterday. Just go at two-thirty and tell them we switched."

She came over and squeezed Shelley's arm. When Shelley stiffened and dropped her juice box, Natalia backed up and took a long drink of water. Then she waved as if she were already a long way off and jogged down the corridor.

By ten, Shelley had eaten half a dry bagel and called every motel in South Dakota within a one-hundred-mile radius of Badlands National Park. David had said they would stay at Motel 6es and she tried every one, testing the patience of at least five different operators in the state. Next she tried Econo Lodge, Howard Johnson, and Best Western before reminding herself that David was not kidnapping Jason. That in all likelihood they'd just pulled off at an independent motel, a Dew Drop Inn or some such thing. Jason would like that more than a chain, she knew.

Late for the tax-group meeting, she rushed through the North Wing but found everyone snacking around the fountain. The pace of the retreat had slowed, it seemed. No one was worried about starting the meeting on time. Spirits were high, clothes were casual.

The cereal display had been knocked over, and Shelley picked a box of Cheerios off the floor. "Is this your work?" Tim Huggins asked. When she stood, he was smiling.

"I thought maybe it was a stray basketball. Has anyone seen the rookies?"

Seth Cooper joined them. He was holding a large cup of steaming coffee and his face looked pink and raw. "I just heard our chapters for the e-commerce treatise are due next week," he groaned. "Next week? Are they kidding us?"

"But Seth," Shelley said. "If you get yours done, with citations and everything, the partners will like you."

Tim laughed, and Seth attempted to mask his annoyance with a smile. "But will they *really* like me, Shelley? I mean, as much as they like you?"

The meeting was in the Spruce Room. The irony of the fact that she was headed into an hourlong meeting about corporate tax in a room named after the spruce while her son and ex-husband were speeding through the part of the country where it grew in glorious profusion was not lost on her. She said so to Latimer, who sat down next to her at the table. "It's funny, isn't it?" she asked. He nodded quickly.

She dumped her Cheerios into an empty water glass so she could eat them without making noise. But when the meeting started, people around the table focused on her glass while Alan Robbins talked about building the international tax practice in the London office. Shelley filled her lungs to suppress her laughter, but this only made the burst when it came more explosive. She turned red.

"I'm sorry," she said. "It's the Cheerios. I'll put them on the floor. Go on, Alan, I'm sorry."

After the meeting, Shelley avoided the stream of people returning to the main lobby. She retreated to a group of sofas in a sterile alcove and feigned an interest in her retreat information folder. There were classes and activities that afternoon organized to foster group togetherness—cooking, wine tasting, paintball—but they weren't obligatory. The paintball group was leaving from the front entrance in half an hour and Shelley thought she might go. The idea of running around the forest hurling wet paint at her colleagues appealed to her, but she worried she would miss Jason if he called again. The final obligation of the retreat was a formal dinner dance that night. When she thought of it, she felt the rising edge of hysteria moving roughly inside her, somewhere near the top of her stomach.

Far down the hallway, Natalia appeared again. Shelley watched nervously as she turned in her direction, walking fast. Behind her was a short woman, almost running to keep up.

"How could you?" Shelley heard the woman say as they approached. "You're a mother. I've seen you with your baby. Don't you know their advertising intentionally targets children?"

"Please," Natalia said. "Stop it. You don't understand what I do."

"You'd be surprised what I understand."

"You're right."

While the woman caught her breath, Natalia turned to Shelley. "She saw my T-shirt," she said without tugging at it or otherwise calling attention to the logo—interlocking *G*s—across her breasts. Shelley was impressed. "It seems she's read in the paper that Garraty & Grimes represents a certain large tobacco company, and this concerns her." Shelley stood reluctantly.

"Are you also a lawyer for Garraty & Grimes?" the woman asked.

"Yes."

"Then you've helped foster the downfall of this country's youth." She had a slight tic at the top of her left cheek.

"I've lost my son," Shelley said, watching the tiny throbbing.

"To drug addiction?" the woman asked.

Natalia turned on her. "For God's sake."

Shelley shook her head and the woman drifted away. Natalia touched Shelley's arm. "I didn't know."

"Well, I lost control of him, anyway. He's gone to live with his father."

Natalia pressed her lips together. "Oh, well that's . . . " She seemed to make her mind up about something. "That's not really the same thing, Shelley, but thanks for getting her off me." She was annoyed, the first time Shelley had ever seen her that way.

———

Shelley spent the afternoon in her room drinking a bottle of the Virginia white wine, chilled this time with ice cubes in the glass. She wondered how her fellow G&G associates were doing. She looked out the window and saw a few pretty pastel groups on the golf course. At two-thirty, she called the spa and told them to give Natalia Jones's appointment to someone else. "Okay. Thank you for calling, Ms. Jones," the spa attendant said. "You're welcome," she replied.

She watched TV for a time, settling into an old Abbott-and-Costello movie, but was nearly asleep when the phone rang.

"Mom?" Jason said.

"Where are you?" she cried, struggling to sit up straight and mute the television.

"Whoa, Mom. What's wrong?"

"I've been so worried. Where are you?"

"South Dakota," he said defensively. "Didn't you get our message?"

"You should come home."

"Mom?"

"I miss you so much. I'm at this horrible retreat, you wouldn't believe this place. It's horrible, it's . . . I don't know how to describe it. There are bowls of mixed nuts everywhere, day and night, and fountains that run constantly surrounded by more food. Everyone goes around in comfy clothes and it looks like we're having a good time, but we're not. We're inmates, corporate inmates. I think you can put corporate in front of anything. Last night we had a corporate dinner with candles that weren't lit. So I went around and lit them all. People probably thought I was crazy, but it was fun."

Jason said, "Are you exaggerating, Mom? Is this a story?"

"No. I really lit all the candles."

"Did you talk to people? You said the retreat was for getting to know more people, for face time."

"Did I say that? Well, I tried."

There was a pause and then he laughed. It was a strange laugh that she didn't recognize, but she could tell he was nervous about what he was going to say next because of the way he cleared his throat. "You know, you say you don't know how to help me, Mom. Well, I don't know how to help you."

This was not him, Shelley thought. This was David. This was David giving him a way to express what she had already begun to suspect was the problem. And they'd only been together four days.

She hadn't realized she was smiling, grinning. Her cheeks ached. On television, Abbott and Costello were beginning their "Who's on First" routine. They looked cheery and fresh in their old-fashioned baseball uniforms. "It's probably true, Jason. I'm sorry. I could do better if you came home."

"Came home, Mom? I'm not even gone yet. I'm not even to Dad's. We're still driving, Mom."

"It feels like you're gone." She knew she had to stop, to back up. "Okay, I'm sorry. Tell me about the sky you saw yesterday. It sounded so beautiful in your message."

He sighed. "Mom, I can't just . . . do that."

"Please, Jason."

"The weather was weird. I've never seen a sky like that." The reticence in his voice would not fade.

"I know you don't remember England," she started, fast, cheerful. "You were too little, but I took you to Hyde Park a lot. The weather was funny. It rained in spells, the clouds moved fast, and sometimes a sunbeam would break through even though it was raining." She hesitated. She couldn't remember why she'd started this. "But the sky isn't big there, not like where you are now, out West."

They were silent a few moments, and then she said, "Do you want to put your dad on?" He didn't answer. He just handed the phone to David.

"How are you?" he asked.

"Not very well."

"We need time," David said. "This is hard."

"Yes, time," she said. "It's just that I don't feel like I have a lot." She heard David turn away from the phone. In the background, Jason was speaking.

"David? What did he say?"

"He says he remembers that you used to call the sun through the rain like that a summer-blink."

She wrapped her hand around her throat. "He remembers that? Could you put him on again?"

"Um, no," David said. "He's on his way out the door. It's hot here, Shelley, and he wants to swim before dinner."

She couldn't tell whether or not this was true. The idea of Jason sitting silent in the room, waiting for her to hang up, made it difficult for her to breathe. But he had remembered their summer-blinks.

"Okay," she said when she could, "I'm going to go now. Good-bye."

Abbott and Costello were nearing the end of the routine, Costello's clothes twisted, his face flushed and sweaty. The heat of humor, Shelley thought, and switched the television off.

———

She stood slowly and started moving about the room. She straightened the bed and laid out her clothes for the dinner dance: a long black dress she'd bought for the retreat, her shoes, her jewelry. She drew the curtains and showered. She brushed her hair and put on makeup. By the time she went downstairs she felt nearly contained. She avoided Martin, however, and ordered a glass of white wine from another young bartender, with whom she did not start a conversation. Surveying the room, she saw that her dress was perfect.

The Peachtree Ballroom was on the ground floor of Potomac Run. No one was seated yet, everyone was still circling for cocktail hour, but Shelley found her table and looked at the place cards. No senior tax partners. No New York partners at all. On her right, the office manager. On her left, a first-year associate. She sat down gingerly. The ballroom had a western exposure but a parking lot abutted the building on this side and she watched a magnificent sunset through the windshield of a Ford Explorer, a red deodorant pine tree dangling above the sun. When Latimer came over to see how she was, she refrained from mentioning it. He asked if she'd had a good weekend, and she smiled. "It's reminded me so much of England," she said. He thought she was joking and patted her shoulder gently. She declined another drink.

When he left, she sat quietly, her hands folded in her lap, and thought about the sky Jason had seen without her. "You have what it takes," she heard from somewhere behind her. And the person to whom it was said must have known what that was because Shelley didn't hear anything else, only laughter.

Paris

VERY LATE AT NIGHT, she hears her husband at his desk in the next room. She wakes to the sound of his typing, the creak of the wooden floorboards beneath his chair. Sitting up, she realizes the storm that had been approaching all day has arrived. A wind has risen and while she watches the rain begins. Drops splash on the sill and bounce into the room through the open window, their paths briefly lit by the street lamp outside. Bursts of air fill the long white curtains, blowing them high into the room, their edges already ragged with damp. She stands and moves to the window. She closes it, pushing down hard with both hands. While the curtains and the sudden silence descend around her like a cape, she holds her elbows gently and squeezes her upper arms against her body. She stares at the rain-glossed street, at the Paris trees whipping about in the wind.

Pulling her robe around her, she walks into her husband's study. He looks up when she enters, his back to the window.

"Did I wake you?" he asks.

"No, the rain."

"It will cool things off."

"The window?" She points. It is wide open and the wind has blown some of his papers to the floor. "I'll get it."

"Don't," he says, standing up suddenly. "Not all the way. The air is nice." He goes to the window while she picks up the fallen pages. She can hear the Bach cello sonatas playing softly from his laptop.

"Would you like some coffee?" she asks.

"No. I'm not going to work much longer."

She starts to go but stops in the doorway. When her husband concentrates, he makes the face he is making now. It is a fiendish sort of grimace; part mirth, part pain. He bares his teeth and squints his eyes. Long wrinkles run along his forehead, down around his eyes, and up from his chin to the tops of his cheeks. He has made this face since he was a boy, concentrating in school, and now a few of the lines are beginning to show faintly even when his face is relaxed. When they were first married, she would interrupt him when she saw his face begin to contort. She thought this would help him stop; she thought he wanted to stop. But there is a connection for him between the face and his ability to concentrate, and her interruptions were only a nuisance.

It is not a good time, she knows, but she shifts her weight in the doorway and clears her throat.

He starts in his chair, then looks up, frowning. "I thought you'd gone back to bed."

"No, not yet," she whispers. Beneath his gaze, she reaches up to smooth her hair. She remembers a time when dishevelment became her. She would wake flushed and bright-eyed any time of night. Now her hair, which changed texture with each of her babies, takes on strange shapes while she sleeps and her eyes grow puffy. She wishes she had organized herself more before starting this, but now it is too late. She drops her hand and decides to begin, to mention the thing she has not been able to

get out of her mind, the idea she's been thinking about for
weeks, even before they arrived. Her plan about staying on in the
flat.

"Staying on?" he says.

Flat does not roll off her tongue, but she chooses it now to
show that after a week in Paris she feels she has a certain afflic-
tion—that's not what she means—*affinity* for the culture. She is
often tongue-tied when she argues with him.

"After we've left?"

Once, she remembers, she said *unmediated* when she'd meant
unmitigated, as in unmitigated suffering. In the middle of the
argument, he'd corrected her. Lightning flashes in the room and
she thinks about the danger of the silent light. The thunder
that follows a beat later doesn't scare her.

His face stretches into an expression of surprise and concern. "And the kids?" He looks hurt, but she knows this face,
too. It is the pain of inconvenience.

A gust of wind blows a sheet of rain against the window.
They both turn. While he is looking away, she says quickly,
"They should go with you. School starts at the end of August."

Her voice has risen and he swivels in his chair with a finger
raised to his lips to remind her that the children are asleep in the
next room. She knows. But she knows, too, that the gesture is a
retaliation. He presses a button on the keyboard and the cello
goes quiet. She allows him the victory, looking down.

His study and the children's bedroom are separated by only
a screen pulled across an archway. The flat is high-ceilinged and
lovely, but the rooms are small and not easy for the four of them
for the month. When he came the first time, alone, this is where
he stayed and his colleagues at the Sorbonne assumed he would
again. He didn't decide until very late that they should all come;

that, this summer—despite the children's protestations—they should all be together. Their daughter will be off to college in a year, their son the next.

The second night in Paris, she walked with him around the Champ de Mars, the park in front of the Eiffel Tower only a block from their flat. She wanted to tell him that she already misses the children's small bodies, that she doesn't know where they've gone. She started to speak, but just then the lights of the Eiffel Tower flickered on against the pale evening sky. She caught her breath and stopped. He hadn't seen the lights; he was thinking about something else. She didn't tell him to look and he didn't ask her to finish. They continued walking in silence, their shoes gently crunching the dirt promenade in the dusk.

Now he stares at a spot on the floor, his head tilted in thought. She knows she should remain quiet. She thinks about going into the kitchen and making herself a cup of coffee. Instead, with the great wrench of unbroken habit, heat rising in her face, she barrels on.

"I'm just talking about a week or two, just to get my bearings."

When he raises his face to her, he looks bewildered and yet, as usual, perfectly calm. Over the years she has hoped he would raise his voice, just once. "He who loses his temper loses the argument," he has always said, and now she hears their daughter, who takes after him, say it to her brother all the time. Their son takes after her and yells at the first touch of temper. Because of it, he will never win an argument against his father or his sister. She makes sure that he gets the best of her sometimes.

"I have no idea what this means, what you want it to mean," he whispers. He closes his laptop and rises from his chair. "The kids will be mystified. But if you can find a way to explain it to them . . . "

"What?" she says, following him into the kitchen. "If I can find a way to explain it to them . . . what?"

Standing at the sink, he drinks a glass of water. When he is finished, he shakes his head.

"You'll support me?" she offers, but her husband, placing the glass carefully on the counter, walks past her into the bedroom.

She will stop, she says to herself. She will let it go for now and talk to him later. She smokes a cigarette by the kitchen window, her eyes slowly adjusting to the dark in the small inner courtyard, not much more than an air shaft. The wind has diminished, but the rain is steady, drumming on something at the bottom of the shaft she cannot see. With a pang she remembers the children's window. She drops her cigarette into the sink and hurries into their room. The sill is soaked and one of her daughter's books ruined. She watches them sleeping; her daughter languid on her back, one slim arm carelessly tossed above her head; her son on his side, somehow still the sleep of a child, his knees up and his curly head tucked into his chest. She would like to wake them. She presses her hands into the cold water on the sill, then presses her palms against her eyes.

Ideas of Home,
but Not the Thing Itself

Andrew and lena easterly were newlyweds and didn't mind that their one-bedroom apartment in Washington didn't have air-conditioning. It was one of the hottest summers on record, but they were young and good-looking; when they got home from work, they just stripped off their clothes. The jet stream seemed inconsequential by comparison, far away and having nothing to do with them. Lena wore a tank top with her underwear, her long waist allowing a band of taut skin to show above her panties. Andrew wore his boxers with a white T-shirt. They made dinner padding around the little galley kitchen barefoot, the soles of their warm feet tacky on the beige linoleum. They ate at a small folding table covered with a daisy-print cloth in jarring colors: red, pink, yellow. It was not theirs. Nothing in the apartment was. They'd rented it furnished.

They were married in May, in Maryland, too late for cherry blossoms and too early for lilac. The lilac in Lena's bouquet was supposed to be white but had arrived only partially in bloom, many buds mature but not yet open, the nascent flowers straining at their enclosing skein. Next to her dress, they had looked lime green.

She had walked alone on the beach toward Andrew, both of them barefoot in the sand, her dress and long veil blowing toward the water. Their families were from the Midwest, and some of them couldn't afford to come, but the wedding was like this and here, on the Chesapeake Bay, because it suited their idea of how a wedding should be: simple, windy, dreamy. No place was dreamy in the Midwest.

They were married by a Unitarian minister who stipulated only two things when they met him for an interview. The first: he would not mention the Trinity. Unitarians did not believe in it. In fact, it was more than that, he said. They believed the concept of the Trinity was responsible for more religious strife than any other single concept in any religion. He grew flushed and fell silent, waiting for their answer.

Lena looked at Andrew, then turned back to the minister and told him this would not be a problem. She was tall and slender, with long blond hair and blond down on her limbs and upper lip. She held her back straight and had a calm, composed manner. They had no strong feelings about the Trinity, she said. They did, however, want to recite the Lord's Prayer. She found it comforting, remembered it fondly as a nighttime prayer from her childhood. Andrew, who was Jewish, thought it largely secular. "Will that be acceptable?" she asked.

"Yes," the minister said. "Of course."

"And we want to break the glass and say *mazel tov*," Andrew added. He was taller than Lena and had sloped shoulders and a soft waist. The beginnings of a belly, Lena often warned, and made him exercise.

"Not a problem," said the minister.

How to break the glass on the sand had been a sticking point. The glass was supposed to be stomped on and broken quickly with a good sound. In the sand, Lena was concerned it would just sink. Her mother, disdainful of many of the wedding arrangements, suggested placing a two-by-four at the feet of the minister and bride and groom.

"Does it have to be a two-by-four?" Lena asked. "Couldn't it be something less utilitarian?"

"Oh, honey," said her mother. "I was joking."

Nevertheless, Lena settled on a square piece of pine. She wanted it to be painted white, and Andrew saw that it was. He forgot to sand the edges, however, and during the ceremony Lena's long veil caught and snagged.

The minister's second stipulation: he would not, like the rest of the wedding party, go barefoot.

———

In the little apartment in Washington, there was a wall decoration Lena disliked, a sun mask made of glazed clay. Brightly painted in hues of red and orange, it looked like something hastily picked up at a souvenir shop. There were long, wobbly rays and the eyelashes above the narrow eye holes stood out in bas-relief. It was a horrible piece and why anyone would want to have it above the kitchen table, arguably the center of the household, Lena said, was a mystery.

Andrew agreed, but said Ms. Gorman, the woman who owned the apartment, lived alone. "Does a woman living alone have a center to her household? Or does the idea imply family?" he asked.

There were other things in the apartment Lena disliked. The mint-green sea horses on the ends of all the curtain rods; the seashells on the coffee-table legs.

"O the futility," she cried, "of decorating your home in a sea theme!" If you're on the shore, she explained to Andrew, the best you can hope for is redundancy. If you're not, then you're only reminding everyone.

"It's like Southwestern in Maine," she said, trying to give him another example. "Hopeless."

In the evenings, Lena and Andrew lounged on the twin turquoise-blue sofas that, crushed in around the seashell coffee table, constituted the living room. They talked about the things they would have in their own house one day. Lena spoke of large rooms, soft sofas, and long billowy curtains, mahogany tables and oriental rugs, antique chairs and doors opening onto grass and light. What they would not have, they agreed, was clutter. They had both come from middle-class, overstuffed homes; houses straining at the seams from all that had been acquired in the pursuit of happiness. None of it, once assembled, had made anything even resembling the original dream. Curtains and carpets were never the right color. Furniture was patched and cleaned over the years, never replaced. It broke their mothers' hearts and confused their tired, disappointed fathers.

One night after dinner, they discussed the little arrangement of plywood boards that formed the only shelving in the apartment, the resting place for a small collection of Oxford classics. Lena objected to the shelving; Andrew pointed out that the books, at least, were good. Lena described the kind of bookshelves they might have one day. She liked natural cherry, possibly in units that could stand alone or together.

"Someday I'd like to have only hardcover books," Andrew said.

"That would be nice," Lena agreed. "Of course, we'll have to leave some room for displaying."

"Displaying?"

"Pictures, and things we collect. Figurines, maybe. Or bowls."

Andrew liked bookshelves with books, but when he mentioned this to Lena she grew upset. He moved over to her sofa and, breathing the sweetness of her skin, murmured that they'd find their own place soon.

In June his parents came to visit. His mother walked in and said, "Oh, isn't this sweet? It's just perfect for you two." She turned to Andrew's father. "I love sea horses! Why didn't we do something like that?"

In July Lena's mother came to visit. She said that if she and Lena's father, who had divorced when she was five, had had such a place their first year, everything might have been different. "Two sofas," she said. "We never could have afforded two sofas."

By August Lena's impatience with the apartment was palpable; every night she announced how many days they had until their sublet ended, every Sunday she pored over the real-estate section of the newspaper. When Karen Boylan, a senior partner at Andrew's company, asked if he'd like to house-sit while she was on vacation for a week with her family, Andrew jumped at the chance. There was a cat, Goldie, but Andrew thought Lena's dislike of cats and his allergic reaction to them were insignificant compared to the opportunity. Lena agreed, and they moved into the large Tudor in Cleveland Park on the second Saturday of

August. It was a muggy afternoon, but when they walked in the front door the air was dry and cool. "Air-conditioning," Andrew breathed and stopped in the doorway to pick up the mail. As he stood, Goldie appeared, an old orange cat with long, wispy fur. She glanced at him, then walked into the kitchen. Andrew's eyes began to itch.

For an hour, Lena moved through the rooms running her hands over the expensive materials, studying the colors and arrangement of things. Andrew trailed behind her. The furnishings were beautiful, antiques and oriental rugs, oils and watercolors decorating the walls, lush furniture in every room. Andrew noticed that the bookshelves contained books and, at intervals, pieces of blue-and-white porcelain. Lena pointed out how all the muted colors and delicate patterns in every room complemented each other. She said this took a great deal of skill and she marveled at Karen's ability.

That afternoon they sunbathed in the backyard and when the air cooled they came in and made an elaborate dinner. Lena said they should dress up and eat in the dining room with candles. Andrew agreed but was not entirely comfortable. The long mahogany table was so polished he could see Lena's reflection moving in the sheen at the far end. His own hands made ghostly imprints on the cool wood. When the candles began to drip on the mahogany, he rushed to wipe up the wax, but Lena laughed. She told him to let the wax cool and harden, then she showed him how to flip it off like a pancake with the tip of a knife. Underneath, the dark wood was unharmed. "See?" she said and kissed him reassuringly.

The Boylans had said that Andrew and Lena should sleep in their bed. This was strange but thrilling, and as they lay down together on the king-size mattress, they stared up at the twelve-foot ceiling. The bed, in the shape of a Scandinavian sleigh, was exactly the kind Lena said she wanted one day. "And the sheets, Andrew." She slid her hands and feet back and forth as if making a snow angel. "Aren't they wonderful? Egyptian cotton."

They fell asleep touching, but later Andrew woke up alone. For a moment he couldn't remember where he was. His eyes strained in the dark, his heart pounded. He slipped a foot from beneath the sheet and when his toe touched the floor, the room spun into the correct orientation and he sat up.

He walked along the upstairs hall, stunned at how cold and quiet the house was. Even the stairs were silent. All the staircases he'd ever known had creaked or groaned. He found Lena in the living room, alert and very still, hugging her knees under a white nightgown on one of the silk sofas.

"I can't wait," she said, glancing around the room. "Do you think they remember the first thing? Say it was the coffee table. How did they choose?" She stared at the piece. "How do you know if it's what you'll want in ten years or twenty or thirty? You might think it doesn't matter. In ten years you'll buy another coffee table if you want to, but life doesn't always work out that way. My parents bought a coffee table, not a very good one, thinking they would replace it someday. They were divorced before the warranty was up. My mom still has it."

Andrew looked at the table. It was low and glossy in the shadows. He imagined it moving, crouching. "I don't think coffee tables have warranties," he said.

"She hates that table."

Andrew noticed Lena's wedding ring in the glow from the window. He twisted his own on his finger and asked if she wanted to come back to bed.

Sunday morning, Lena rearranged the kitchen. The set of antique canisters was lost behind the sink, she explained to Andrew when he walked in. She'd moved them to the counter. And some decorative Dutch and Portuguese tiles behind the stove looked much better in the Welsh cabinet.

The pajamas Andrew was wearing were flannel and not his. Lena had found them in Mr. Boylan's dresser after their midnight talk and he'd put them on, too cold and tired to protest. Now he pulled nervously at the sleeves.

Lena took a leaf out of the table and shoved the two halves together with a grunt. She put fresh flowers from the garden in a vase. "Beautiful," she said, standing back for a moment to survey her work. "I feel like I've come up for air. We were drowning in that apartment."

"Are you sure it's okay to cut their flowers?" he asked.

"They'd be dead by the time they got back."

"Lena, what are you doing?"

"It's just for fun," she said. "We'll put everything back." She took a small, framed watercolor from the kitchen out into the hall and started on the living room.

Andrew stood in the kitchen. Goldie came in and walked over to the place where her food bowl had been. She sniffed the floor delicately and looked up at Andrew. They eyed each other until Andrew's nose began to fill.

Lena moved furniture in every room, but nothing was damaged or scratched. Goldie seemed disturbed by the activity and had started to shed profusely, but by Monday morning had stopped racing from room to room. Andrew's nose was permanently stuffed, but on Tuesday his eyes stopped itching. Lena was happy. The week, it seemed to Andrew, was going well.

Wednesday night Andrew came home late from work and found Lena watching television on the floor of the Boylans' family room. From the jumpiness of the scenes and the quality of the color, he could tell it was not a program but some sort of home video. There were many well-dressed people milling around, frequently hugging, in front of a church. Then there was a shot of a nervous-looking bride surrounded by a group of pink bridesmaids.

"It's their wedding," Lena said.

"Should you be watching it?" Andrew asked.

"Why not? I found the tape in the drawer beneath the television."

"It seems weird."

"They asked us to house-sit."

"Right. Not watch their private videos."

"It's not private. It's their wedding." She leaned forward to rest her chin on her knee. "Don't watch, then," she said.

"I won't. I'm going to get a drink." In the kitchen, Andrew opened a beer and heated his dinner. When a trumpet and organ recessional drifted out to him, he carried his food into the family room. He suspected that watching the wedding of two people he barely knew would be strange. What he hadn't anticipated was that Lena would compare everything to their own wedding. Why hadn't they thought of irises for the tables? She loved irises. Were those real pearls? She hadn't known you could do that with tulle. A church wedding was so nice. She loved the music.

Why hadn't they thought to have music during the ceremony?

"I really don't see the point of this," Andrew said finally. "I liked our marriage. What is the good of thinking now about how you would do it differently?"

Lena was silent a moment. On the screen, the bride and groom began their first dance.

"But that's just it," she said. "I would do things differently."

"So? That doesn't mean anything."

"I don't know."

"It doesn't. We had a nice marriage."

"No, we had a wedding, the kickoff, the celebration. The marriage comes after, fifty years of in-sickness-and-in-health, the life plan."

"Fine. We're still married, then. Is that better?"

"No," Lena said, sitting up suddenly. "I don't know if it is." She grabbed the remote and pushed the pause button. The young Mr. and Mrs. Boylan froze on the screen in trembling lines, trapped in an embrace on an empty dance floor.

Andrew and Lena made up immediately. They kissed and talked in whispers, the reconciliation of their first real argument too precious and tender for full volume. Then they were standing in the Boylans' bedroom, kissing between apologies, between sentences, in the middle of words. They had not made love in the bed, neither of them completely comfortable with the idea. But it did seem that if you asked someone to house-sit and insisted they should sleep in your bed, you had probably thought of the possibility and didn't mind.

"Don't you think?" Lena whispered.

"I do," Andrew said. "I do. And you said she definitely wanted us to sleep in their room. Right? She said it twice?"

"Right," Lena said.

Standing at the foot of the bed, they undressed quickly. When Andrew felt something soft against his ankles, he sneezed; Goldie had come into the room. He bent down, but Lena quickly scooped her up and put her out. Andrew was astonished and enormously grateful. Lena didn't usually touch cats.

He looked at her, surprise and love stinging his eyes. "You're wonderful. Let's never grow old and set in our ways."

"But, Andrew," Lena said. "That's one of the problems. We don't have any ways."

Their last night at the Boylans, they ate dinner outside. They sat in the garden, drank wine, and listened to a ball game on the radio. Andrew was content. "Someday," he said, stretching in his chair, and Lena smiled.

But when they went inside to move everything back, Lena said she couldn't really remember where everything had been. She hadn't made a list. For a few desperate moments, Andrew stood paralyzed in the middle of the living room. What would the Boylans do? Could Karen fire him for rearranging her house? Where had the set of stacking cherry side tables been?

Lena, calmly dusting some vases on the mantel, suggested there was a chance the Boylans might like the change. "I think what I've done is good," she said.

Andrew stared.

"We've been happy here," she continued. "People say you're not happy if you have everything you want, but this house is everything we want and we've been happy."

"It's not ours," Andrew said. "We're happy the way people are happy when they stay in a luxury hotel. It's not real."

"But it is real. Nice things make people happy. Why else are there museums?"

"This isn't our house," he said again, insisting on it, feeling the argument slipping away from him.

They replaced what they could and slept that night under a blanket on top of the washed and ironed sheets. Andrew lay awake a long time, the silence of the house growing large around him. Once, he thought he heard Goldie scratching in the hall.

———

When they opened the door of Ms. Gorman's apartment the next afternoon, there was a notice from the manager on the floor. Something had arrived earlier than expected and he would bring it up for them when they called.

"Do you know what it is?" Andrew asked.

Lena was unpacking their things. "Oh, something I ordered, I think."

Within the hour, a wingback chair identical to one in the Boylan house, although in white watermarked silk instead of beige, was sitting in the middle of the apartment. Andrew shoved Ms. Gorman's bright sofas out of the way to make room. The chair, in comparison, seemed sophisticated and calm. Pure white surrounded by cheap color.

Lena and Andrew sat next to each other on one of the sofas. "I like it," Andrew said.

"I was going to tell you."

"When?"

It was hot and still in the apartment and where their knees touched the skin stuck and began to sweat. They moved apart, wiping their legs. Andrew did like the chair. It seemed a good choice for a first major acquisition; basic white, it would go with everything. He hoped they could afford it. He turned to ask Lena, but saw her eyes filling with tears.

"I made a mistake," she said. "The beige was better."

Andrew looked back at the chair. He wasn't sure there was all that much difference. "It doesn't matter. We can return it."

"No," Lena said. "It was on sale."

"Well, I like it," he said after a minute, trying to sound confident and reassuring. "I think it's perfect for us."

Lena shook her head furiously.

They went to bed early that night. While Lena was getting ready, Andrew tried to think of a way to cheer her up. He remembered the sun mask and took it down from the wall. Holding it before his face, he walked to the bathroom. He would surprise her, he thought. He would dance, she would laugh, and they might shower together before bed. But he'd forgotten that the door to the bathroom was opposite the fish-shaped mirror trimmed in pink seashells over the sink. Their eyes met in the mirror and Lena paused, brush in mouth. She frowned. Andrew stood still. It seemed to him that the entire situation, except for the pink fish mirror, was like something out of a horror film, the villain viewed in the mirror behind the heroine. Lena looked away and resumed brushing more vigorously than before. Andrew, regretting his plan but feeling he was probably too far in to abandon it, went ahead with the dance. After one circuit around the bathroom, he hopped out and closed the door quietly behind him.

When he climbed into bed, Lena curled away from him.

"Sweetheart," he said, although he'd never called her that before and the word rang strangely in his head. "We'll find our way," and he crawled over awkwardly to give her a hug.

First Sale

THE BOY KICKS the apartment door open with the toe of his sneaker, lets it fall back, kicks it again. It's the end of a hot summer and he's waiting for his mother, who has slept late. He's dressed himself in shorts and a blue T-shirt. He's eaten a bowl of cereal, mixing the last of several boxes, and watched television most of the morning. Now he calls to her, impatiently, and she comes, walking slowly, her head down. She frowns as if trying to remember something. While he watches, she stops and looks for something in her purse.

"What's taking so long?"

"Go ahead," she says.

He runs down the hallway. He can reach the elevator button now and so stretches up to do it. Holding this position, smiling over his shoulder, he waits for her to round the corner. He looks down at the ashtray between the elevator doors, at the butts and black stains in the white sand.

"Look!" he cries when his mother appears and stretches taller on his toes.

She leans over and pushes a half-finished cigarette into the sand. "Good," she says, exhaling smoke.

He pushes the button and comes down heavily on his heels. "What's the name again?"

She sighs. "I can't keep telling you. Newfound Lake."

His father left Washington a few days ago for this place where the boy's uncle lives in New Hampshire. Before he left, he gave the boy a fishing pole and tackle box. He said that next year they would go fishing together, and the boy has started practicing from his bed.

In the cool damp air of the basement, she asks the building manager, Mr. Wallace, if they can have a yard sale on the building's front walk. He stares at them. No one has ever used the front walk of the Queensborough for a sale, he says. The boy can smell his perspiration, a sharp smell like his father's after he walks home from work.

We need to pare down, she says, and it would be a shame to throw the things away. She tells him people had yard sales all the time where she grew up. Sometimes the whole neighborhood would pitch in. The boy hears her voice change tone, grow warm and more lively. He looks eagerly at Mr. Wallace, hoping he will ask her something more.

Instead, he opens a drawer at the side of his desk. "How old are you? Twenty-eight? How much stuff could you have?"

"Enough," she says, her voice flat again.

"Where do you think you're going to put everything?" Mr. Wallace asks.

We'll keep everything on the walk and front patio, she says, and leave a path open to the front door at all times.

"Want a piece?" Mr. Wallace rises suddenly and leans across the desk, offering a crushed pack of gum.

Mr. Wallace unwraps a piece of gum for himself. "Isn't a yard sale the same thing as a garage sale?" he says. "You need to find a proper garage." He grins broadly, pleased with this solution, and slaps the desk.

The boy sees his mother jump at the noise. "We don't have a garage," he volunteers quickly. He's worried about her and the day. She said this would be a fast stop, but he has felt it become, like many things in the past few weeks, strangely difficult.

The manager stops chewing and swallows. "Don't look that way, little guy. You can have your sale."

They settle on a week from the day, the first Saturday in September, and his mother thanks him and leaves the office. When they are out in front of the Queensborough, momentarily dazed by the bright sun, the boy says, "He was mean." She doesn't answer, and he looks down and kicks the ground. "Grandma had yard sales?"

She has her sunglasses on now and is lighting a cigarette. She starts down the stairs and he steps quickly after, reaching for her hand, as he often does, to remind her of him.

———

When he wakes the next morning, his yellow curtains are already soft with sun and the pigeons are cooing on his windowsill. He worries she's started without him. He jumps out of bed and runs to her room, realizing on the way that she's still asleep. The apartment is quiet. There are no breakfast noises or smells. There are no boxes packed. He stops running and walks the last steps to her door. Pushing it open, he stands in the door frame, very still. The quilt lies crumpled in a chair and the overhead light is on.

She snores softly, her lips coming apart to make a wet puffing sound with each exhale. He calls to her, twice, loudly, wanting the noise to stop.

She groans and rolls over.

He says, "I thought we were going to pack for the sale."

"We are."

"When?"

"Soon. I'm tired. I was up late talking to your father."

"You were?"

"Yes. We talked—" She stares in his direction, waking up more as she focuses on him. "He's having a nice time fishing. Go have some cereal and I'll be up in a bit."

"Has he caught anything?"

"I don't know."

"He didn't tell you?"

"I guess he forgot. Go on."

In the kitchen there is no cereal or milk but he doesn't feel like eating. In a stack in the corner there are some boxes his mother has collected from the Safeway across the street and Cairo, the package store next door. He looks at them a minute, then picks out a small one and takes it into the living room. Standing in his pajamas, the box dangling at his side, he looks around at their belongings, at the brown corduroy sofa, the end tables draped in shawls, the wobbly bookshelves, the overstuffed chair and ottoman. There is a square coffee table with a glass top and a shelf underneath cluttered with newspapers and magazines. Against the far wall, his mother's spinet piano stands next to a small cabinet holding the television and stereo. To his left, behind the sofa, is a window that looks out over the flat gray roof of the Safeway.

He bounces the box against his knee. He has no idea what to pack. All of it seems necessary to him, all of it familiar and indispensable. He's about to abandon the job when his mother walks into the room. She has pulled on jeans and a black tank top; her shoulders are bony and tan.

"Come on," she says. "I'll show you."

She begins picking up things. "Anything we don't use any-more and is just taking up space. For example, these coasters? We never have parties."

She whirls around with the coasters in her hand. He stares at her, then lifts the box slightly and she tosses them in, one by one, like Frisbees, each time stylishly flicking her wrist. They hit the bottom with a hollow sound. When she finishes they are both quiet, staring at the discs in the box.

She smiles at him briefly, then runs a hand through her hair and walks to the far end of the room. She pulls records and CDs off the shelves and drops them on the floor at her feet.

"What about books?" he asks.

"Oh, yes," she says. "Especially your father's."

"Which ones?"

She turns and studies him. "Never mind," she says. "I can do that part. Why don't you just help me with your things. Go through your room and figure out what you don't need any-more. You can keep the money from what you sell."

He thinks about this. "I don't want to sell anything," he says.

She turns away.

"I could think about it," he offers, but she is throwing paper-backs to the floor and doesn't answer. The sunlight has bright-ened since the early morning and there is much yellow in it. He hears cars on the street below and people laughing. It feels strange to be inside, holding a box. He turns when his mother, stepping out of the mound she has created around her, slips on a book and almost falls.

She fills the boxes quickly and loosely, then pushes or kicks them across the floor. She is working hard, fast, talking to herself. The boy has been to his room and looked through his things. He has collected some unused coloring books and a few matchbox cars he no longer favors. When he came out to show his mother, he found her throwing clothes out of her closet. He hadn't thought of clothes. He went back to his room and pulled out the red snowsuit he has worn for several winters. He folded it carefully and placed it neatly in his box.

Now he trails her around the apartment. The surfaces of everything seem bare to him, all the pretty boxes, picture frames, and vases lying in boxes or on the floor. He sees nicks and stains he's never noticed, and hollow squares of dust, the outlines of removed things. When she is working in the small den where his father sleeps he asks once more if he can help. His mother, leaning deep into a box, tells him there is nothing he can do.

He plays by himself for a while until, overheated, the blood pounding in his ears, he stops and lies on his back in the middle of the living room. The cardboard boxes have filled the humid air with a cloying, sweet scent. He rubs his nose to rid it of the smell. Soon the humming in his ears subsides and he realizes with a start that the apartment is very quiet. He scrambles up and runs from the room, calling.

He finds his mother curled up on the chair in her room. "I fell asleep," she says when he appears, breathless, in the doorway. She blinks a few times, then pushes the hair out of her eyes. "What've you been doing?"

"Playing," he says, his stomach tight. He pulls at his pajama top, tugging it out and away from him, balling his fists inside. "Why are you sleeping?"

"I got tired."

"Why are you tired?"

She looks down and does not answer. "Are you hungry?" she asks suddenly. "Should we have lunch?"

He shrugs and they are both quiet.

"Come sit?" she asks softly and pats her lap.

He leaves the doorway slowly, stepping carefully over the things on the floor.

"Well, never mind if it's such a chore," she says sharply.

"It's okay," he says and hurries to her.

———

In his room he presents his orderly box. She makes him try on the snowsuit and when the sleeves don't reach his wrists she sighs and tells him he can take it off. Then she looks at his box again and agrees there may be nothing else, but she wants to make sure. She kneels in his closet, and he plops down on the bed.

"This?" she says, stretching an arm behind her. Between two fingers she holds a little corked bottle filled with water from the place in Maryland where they spent a weekend the summer before.

"I want that!" he shouts.

She stands and turns around, the bottle still in her hand. "Oh, honey," she says and she is looking at him, but then she isn't. He knows this trick of her gaze. Her eyes redden and she focuses on a place above his head.

"Would someone buy it?" he asks.

She blinks and looks at him. "Maybe. You never know what people will want."

"Okay," he says.

She smiles sadly and gives him the bottle. "No, you should keep it. They're your memories."

The bottle is square and made of clear glass with a picture of a crab etched into the front. His father bought it for him at a store in town their last afternoon. When they got back to the cabin, the boy waded into the water until it came up to his knees. His parents were standing behind him on the shore, and when he'd been out there a long time they called to him.

It won't fit the whole bay, his father said.

I know, he answered.

What're you doing, honey? his mother asked.

Scooping the sunlight, he explained.

And his parents had laughed. He understood then that it was impossible, but he liked their laughing and he liked the idea that he could make them laugh. Standing in the path of sunshine bouncing on the water, he had turned toward them and scooped and splashed some more.

Now he shakes the bottle. A bit of sand swirls up from the bottom, but the water looks brown and dull. "No," he says. "It's okay, but I don't see why anyone would want it." He slides off the bed and puts the bottle gently in the box for the sale.

In the week before the yard sale, morning becomes night and night day. They eat eggs for dinner and sandwiches for breakfast; they are often awake at midnight and asleep at noon. They eat at the coffee table in the living room, the kitchen table too roomy, she says, for just the two of them. He tries to set their places the way she used to, scrupulously folding white paper napkins into triangles and placing the fork and knife neatly on top. They sit Indian-style on pillows on the floor.

"Isn't this more fun?" she asks, and he watches her across the table and nods.

She sleeps late in the mornings, but at night she moves about. He hears her in the kitchen, at the piano. She plays softly, humming over the notes in broken phrases. A few times he hears her footsteps outside his door.

As the sale approaches, he does everything he can to help. She says it will be fun, but he just wants it to go well, to achieve the expectations she seems to have for it. He searches his room and finds more things to sell, some puzzles and games, a few toys.

Twice the boys from the building come by and ask him to play, but he refuses. He wants to stay home. He feels vigilant, brave, necessary. It is early September, the days already shorter and the apartment, much to his consternation, always in dim half-light. He walks from room to room in the early evening while his mother sleeps, turning lights on everywhere, trying to banish with electric light whatever has changed her so.

"Negotiate anything, get rid of everything. That will be the motto of the day," she says cheerfully, holding a pen in her mouth while she peels off a sticker. It is the day of the sale and she has brushed her hair and pulled it back into a soft fresh ponytail. She was up this morning before him and he thinks she looks wonderful. When she sees him looking at her, she explains that negotiate means being willing to compromise. He nods gravely and returns to his work.

Flanked by two patches of lawn, the front walk is seven side-walk squares across by eight squares deep. On the left, three steps lead up to a narrow patio and the Queensborough's front door. Carpeted in bright green plastic, the patio runs the width of the walk and is as high as the boy's waist. On this ledge he sets in decreasing size from left to right several pairs of old shoes, starting with a pair of his father's and finishing with his own winter boots. In between are a couple pairs of his mother's shiny heels. She waits patiently for him to finish, her hand on her hip, a funny smile on her face.

"They look great," she says when he is done and tousles his hair. "Now help me with the other things."

They spread an old blanket on the right side of the walk, and although the morning is still and hot, he anchors every corner with rocks he has picked out of the lawn border. They fold the clothing into neat rows and set out the other small items, all labeled now with prices. The furniture stands in a row on the opposite side of the walk, leaving a path open, as promised, to the steps and the front door.

When everything is ready, they sit on the patio ledge next to the shoes and survey the scene. The whole area shimmers in bright morning sun. The squares of lawn glisten with the last of the dew, and the ferns that line the walk move slowly in a barely discernible breeze. Pots of pink and red geraniums at either end of the patio fill the area with a humid fragrance. The boy doesn't know where all these things from his home have been kept, but now, arranged in this way in the open air and sunshine, they look fine to him. It is eight o'clock, and people are beginning to move about the neighborhood. An old man pushes his shopping cart toward the Safeway; Mr. Cusano, the owner of the coffee shop across the street, comes out and waves to the boy.

"You know him?" his mother asks.

"Yes," he answers, feeling important.

He looks at his mother and thinks about the course of the day, how the whole of it will be spent in this space. He's relieved to be out of the apartment, relieved that she seems happy. Even though they can run upstairs if they have to, she has said they should make it feel like a day out, like an adventure. She has packed a lunch for them and a bag of things to do.

———

By the time the cicadas start, filling the damp air with the sound of heat, the sale has been going an hour and a half. They have sold nothing. Sitting on the ledge, bouncing his heels nervously against the wall, he watches his mother out of the corner of his eye. She reads a magazine and the morning wears on. People come and go, some stop to browse, but no one buys anything. He concentrates on every person who passes.

Then a young woman walking a dog stands a long time looking at the dresser and rocking chair. When she turns to speak to his mother, the dog jumps up on the boy's legs. He starts to push him down, but when he sees his mother stand and smile at the girl, he holds the dog's paws and lets him lick his hands. The girl decides to buy both pieces. She has just graduated from college and moved to the city with her boyfriend. She and his mother talk for a while about college and moving, first apartments and jobs. Then his mother says she won't take more than thirty dollars for both things, even though the original price was twenty for each.

"Save your money," she says. "You never know when it might be useful to have some of your own."

More time passes without a sale, but the boy feels at ease. He starts a new coloring book and his mother returns to her magazine. Occasionally, she gets up to straighten things browsers have displaced and gradually they sell more, his mother handling all the sales and keeping the money in an envelope in her pocket. She smiles at everyone who turns off the sidewalk, and she thanks each person who takes away something that was theirs.

At one o'clock she says it is time for lunch, and they move into the shade of the ginkgo tree on the city apron. While she unwraps his sandwich, she asks him if there's anything he's looking forward to about going back to school next week. He feels the weight of her attention and wants to answer well.

"I hope the beekeeper comes again."

She looks at him, puzzled.

"He came last year and told us about bees. He petted the fur on its back and—"

"I don't remember this. Someone brought a bee into your classroom?"

"Yeah. A bumblebee. We could pet it, if we wanted."

"Did you?"

Remembering his fear, he looks down. "No," he says quietly.

She says it must have been an interesting demonstration, but he should be careful, that it was probably a special kind of bee and not like the ones outside.

"But," he insists, "the man said bumblebees don't want to sting. He put it in his mouth and let it fly off his tongue." Seeing her expression, he rushes on. "He did. Just like this. Watch." He breaks off a piece of pretzel. "This is the bee," he says, cupping the bit of pretzel in his hand, then popping it into his mouth. A few seconds later, he opens his mouth and sticks out the tip of his tongue. The pretzel balances there unbroken.

"That's just how he did it," he finishes, chewing quickly and swallowing.

She laughs and the boy, pleased, talks faster. "The bee stayed there for a second, kind of looking around, and the beekeeper rolled his eyes as a joke, and then it flew away."

He hopes she will ask more questions—there's a lot to tell her about the bee, he realizes—but she's quiet now and looks away.

"I should see if he needs any help," she says, getting to her feet. "He ran by earlier."

A tall man dressed in running shoes and shorts is looking at the books on the blanket. The boy watches him over the line of his sandwich, which he holds in front of him, his elbows propped on his knees. The man picks up one of the large hardcovers and starts to open it at the same time his mother tries to wipe some dust off the front cover. They fumble and the book totters and almost falls to the ground. They both laugh. With the book successfully open and secure in his hands, the man begins talking, occasionally shifting the book to one hand and pointing at the page with the other. His mother stands quietly, her head tipped slightly to one side.

The boy finishes his sandwich and opens the box of cookies. He eats three, one more than he is allowed. A few minutes later his mother turns to check on him, and he quickly hides his fourth. She waves, then takes a few steps with the runner toward the patio. They rest the book on the ledge next to the shoes and lean over it, his mother flipping through the pages now, too, talking and pointing. The boy concentrates on his coloring, leaning close over his crayon, warm and waxy in his hand without its paper. He grips it hard, making red half-moons beneath

his fingernails. People pass near him and through his eyelashes
he keeps an eye on the ones who stop to look at the sale.

Some time later, he wakes from a sweaty nap. The shade of
the tree has shifted and he and the remains of the picnic are in
full sun. Sitting up, he looks over and sees his mother and the
man still talking, the book closed now and tucked under his
arm. People are returning from picnics and pool outings, many
with fresh sunburns across their shoulders and noses. Mr. Wallace steps out and stands on the corner of the patio. He looks
at the sale and seems to measure with his eyes the amount of
room people have to go in and out. He raises an eyebrow, first
at the boy, then at the boy's mother, who doesn't notice. Eventually he shakes his head and walks back into the building.

The boy stands up and begins straightening and reorganiz-
ing. Many things are gone and he's able to fit what remains into
a smaller space, hoping this will prevent Mr. Wallace from saying anything to his mother. He picks up the little bottle. Pre-
tending to move it from one place to another, he slips it quietly
into his pocket.

While he is straightening, he hears the man and his mother
saying good-bye. He thanks her for the book; she says she has
enjoyed talking; they both say how glad they are to have met.
Then, hearing their voices go quiet behind him, he turns.

He sees the man reach out and touch his mother's arm. He
sees her smile and blush and put her hand over his.

———————————

The boy plucks at the green plastic carpet, his chin propped
on his knee. Sitting on the far side of the patio, he is away from

the shoes, away from the sale. When the runner is gone, however, his mother comes over. "How's the sleepyhead?" she asks, sitting down next to him.

He doesn't look at her, but a question rushes fiercely out of him. "Do you know him?"

"The man I was talking to? No, I just met him today. He bought an old art book of your father's."

"You didn't finish your lunch," he says, looking up, not able to stop now, his throat hot and tight.

"I wasn't that hungry," she says softly. "You did a good job, though. I saw you."

He shakes his head. "I had four cookies."

"That's okay. Today's special."

She smiles at him, her eyes sparkling. Her bangs are curly and damp around her face, her cheeks rosy with sun.

"Why is it special? Why do people have sales?"

"Oh, lots of reasons. To make a little money, to clear out old things. It's a way of starting over, honey." She puts her arm around his shoulders and tries to pull him close, but he resists.

He turns from her and stares at the geraniums, at a bumblebee moving among the blooms. "Look," he says quickly, and, almost without thinking, reaches out and touches the yellow and black fuzz. The bee moves under his finger and the pitch of the buzzing deepens. He pulls back and the bee flies to another flower farther away. He turns to his mother, his eyes wide.

"Be careful," she says, patting his knee, but he searches her eyes and sees that they are dull again and far away.

The sun drops behind the Queensborough and the shadow of the building begins to creep over the walk. He looks around at the last of their sale, caring about each thing that is left and wanting everything back. The dresser, the picture frames, the puzzles, the clothes—all of it came from the time before, he thinks, and then he understands that there was a time before, when the days were brighter and different. He closes his hand over the bottle in his pocket. He wants to show her, to tell her he kept it, but just then she takes his other hand and lifts it into her lap.

"My brave boy," she says absently and begins stroking the soft underside of his forearm in a long line from his elbow to his wrist. At first it tickles and he wriggles a bit, but she's preoccupied and doesn't notice. He sits still then, not wanting her to stop.

Pantomime

NAN SAID everyone should have a martini in her honor. It was the only time she said anything about what we should do. We argued about whether she was serious, but in the end we had a party and everyone had a martini.

When the friends and neighbors were gone, we took Nan's ashes and two candles to the end of the garden. She was a gardener and she loved the forest, so we buried her where the two meet behind her house. We all helped dig the grave. Dad started with a shovel, then the rest of us got down on our knees and dug with our hands. The Aunts were next to each other, each trying to outdig the other. One said she wanted to sift Nan's ashes through her fingers. She yelled that she wanted to mix them in the dirt with her bare hands. She'd had three or four martinis in Nan's honor.

I'd left school early that year to be with Nan. I was cooking for her and putting in the spring plantings. But then the Aunts came, Nan's daughters. A succession of friends called or visited. Dad came—Nan's only son—and Mom soon after. I spent more time in the garden. Nan spent more time in bed.

One day one of the Aunts said, "You can see her now."

"How is she?" I asked.

"Quiet."

"Does she need anything? Should I bring her breakfast?"

"No," the Aunt said. "Go ahead."

"Thanks. I haven't had much time with her lately."

"I'll be up in a minute," the Aunt said.

When I was little, I had visited Nan every summer. In the mornings, she was always awake before me. I'd run downstairs and we'd go out in our nightgowns to snap off the dead daylilies. Now I walked quietly and stopped in the doorway. Her white nightgown was yellowed at the neck, but her long white hair was washed and brushed and spread out over the pillows. She peered at me over her black-rimmed glasses and smiled. Enormously.

Later, I asked her, "Nan, do you like him?"

"He seems very nice," she said. "We should have had him up here more often. I thought he enjoyed reading by the pond."

"He did. He liked it here very much."

"I remember when the two of you visited and we took breakfast down to Ely's ferry. We had to eat in the car because of the wind."

"You drove right up on the sand so we could see the waves."

"Did I?"

I said, "I think I'm going to marry him, Nan."

She said, "I know."

The next time I sat on the bed with her, I couldn't stop looking at myself in the mirror. Quick glances across the room when her attention was elsewhere. Profile, three-quarter face. Finally I turned so I could see only Nan. Tried to focus on what was happening to her. Later an Aunt said she knew why Jews cover mirrors after a death.

She said, "Nan has noticed, you know."

I said, "What are you talking about?"

She said, "You're old enough to know."

"You're wrong!" I said.

"Then why are you upset?"

When Nan couldn't come downstairs anymore, we needed something to do at night. I went to the video shop down the hill, a small family-owned place. Walking through the door, I remembered a conversation I'd overheard many summers ago.

"Do you remember my daughter?" the owner, Mr. Scott, had asked Nan. "Tall, blond, worked with me weekends?"

"Yes, of course I do," she said.

"Would you come to her memorial service tomorrow? At the Congregational church on Grassy Hill?"

"Memorial service? What happened?" Nan's hands had been moving about in her full purse, searching for the correct change. Now she froze and looked at him steadily.

"She had a heart condition." Just before he covered his face, his mouth trembled, then gaped into a silent sob.

"Oh, Adam," Nan said. I'd never heard his first name. Below the counter, Nan reached for my hand.

———

One day Dad and I were sitting with Nan and she read to us from her journals.

"Put the bulbs in this morning. After lunch, walked with Peggy in the state forest near Uncas Pond. I told her about the bluebird nest in the garden and got so excited I whirled around in front of her and said, 'Oh, Piggy!' It was an accident, of course, but I thought it was very funny. Peggy was offended, I think."

She had to stop reading she was laughing so hard.

The next day I asked her, "What do you dream about, Nan?" It was morning, early. I was alone with her before the Aunts woke up.

She said, "Birds and flowers, usually. I dream about flowers and what kind of bird I would be. What would you be?"

Nan's favorite bird was the cardinal. She could whistle the song perfectly. "A cardinal," I said.

"I used to think so, too, but now I'd like to be a hawk. They can soar for miles on wind currents without flapping their wings. Of course, they're predators," she winked, "which will take some getting used to."

"I'll be a hawk, too." I held her hand.

"That'll be nice. Then we won't be lonely."

"Nan, there's something I want to tell you. I've been looking in the mirror a lot."

She said, "That's all right."

She said, "Girls your age want to look nice."

I said, "Nan! That's not it."

She squeezed my hand and closed her eyes.

Some time after that we were all in the kitchen very late. We faced one another from the four corners of the room: the Aunts together against the stove, Mom smoking by the sink, Dad leaning against the pantry door. I stood in the doorway.

"I think she should be in a hospice." Dad.

"No. Absolutely not." The Aunts.

"We can't make her comfortable here anymore." Mom.

"And you think she'd be more comfortable in a hospice?" The Aunts again. "She hates hospitals."

"I think an emergency might happen here that we can't handle." Dad.

"What kind of emergency? We have everything under control." The Aunts.

"It's awful to think about, but we have to." Mom.

Everyone was quiet. Mom tapped ashes into the sink.

I said, "We could ask the hospice to send a nurse here. I think they do that."

Upstairs we heard Nan's bed creak. One of the Aunts shifted and her butt clicked on one of the gas burners. She whipped around to shut it off. "Fine," she said.

Nan's morphine was increased. The nurse recommended television to help her focus. The Aunts hated the nurse but did what she said. We pulled the TV close to the bed and watched sitcom reruns.

Dinner grew complicated. One night Dad stayed outside. He leaned against the stone wall at the edge of the lawn. In the dark the tip of his cigar made slow orange streaks from his mouth to his waist. Mouth, waist. Rhythmic. Quiet.

I rested my head on the table. In front of me, Mom and the Aunts were preparing Nan's tray. The kitchen light was the only one on in the house.

"She likes her napkin folded in a triangle." Chapped fingers refolding.

"She always has a sprig of parsley on her plate." Refrigerator door flung open.

"She likes her toast in four pieces." Knife screeching against china.

"She always uses the blue mug." Brown one slammed back on the shelf.

Outside the cigar went out, Dad's shape a gathering of darkness along the wall. My eyes went out of focus, refocused on the dark window, my reflection.

All three of them said, "I'll take the tray up."

Once we tried eating dinner in Nan's room. We surrounded her bed, perched on different pieces of bedroom furniture, trays on our laps.

We turned the television off. Nan didn't seem to mind. She rolled her head on the pillow and smiled weakly.

We ate slowly at first, then more quickly, our silverware clinking against Nan's china. Dad told her about the garden, said the abelia was in bloom. I told her the daylilies were starting. Out of the corner of my eye, I saw a cardinal fly past the window.

"Nan, did you see?"

Her gaze moved slowly in the direction of my voice.

"Maybe we should turn on the TV," one of the Aunts said. She slid off the dresser. When the sound came on, Nan rolled her head toward it.

A little while after that we packed a bag for Nan. We were in her bedroom, fans set up all over the place to make her more comfortable. It was summer now and hot. One by one the Aunts carried Nan's nightgowns out of the closet and held them up for her to choose. She nodded at all of them and frowned when they blew in front of the TV.

Then I was holding Nan's hand. Mom was crying. The Aunts were hovering around the bed. Dad was holding papers and a pen. He tried to guide Nan's hand, but she frowned and rolled her head.

One of the Aunts opened a box on her dresser. In it was the jewelry I had seen Nan wear on fancy occasions, holidays. The Aunts started passing things out.

"What're you doing?" I said.

I thought Nan squeezed my hand. The Aunt with the box walked to the bed and handed me a ring with blue and white stones. Not letting go of Nan's hand, I slid it onto my ring finger and held it up for her to see.

The ambulance drove up the hill to the house. The gravel road grumbled so loudly under its weight that I knew it was coming before I saw it through the trees. I yelled to Dad, then ran behind the house. I squatted by the pond, ready to run, but only my fingers moved, tearing blades of grass into tiny pieces that fell on the water without rippling the surface. I could hear the sounds of the paramedics bringing Nan downstairs, out the front door, into the ambulance. I heard the Aunts decide to go with her. I heard Dad decide not to. Then I grabbed a daylily and ran around the side of the house.

I got there in time to see the white metal doors being latched shut.

———

The moonlight was so bright our shadows bumped and clawed each other as we dug. Mozart's Requiem, Nan's favorite, drifted to us from the house. When we were done we stepped back and Dad poured Nan's ashes from the urn into the moist earth. He had chosen the place, Mom had thought of the candles and music, the Aunts had made the deviled eggs and martinis. No one had thought of words. After a while I said, "She would be happy. She loved this spot."

I said, "Flowers will always bloom on her grave."

One of the Aunts snorted, but Dad bowed his head, then knelt down and covered her ashes with the earth and leaves. When he was finished, the forest floor looked undisturbed. We stood for a moment, all of us staring at the hidden place, then we headed back up to the house. Mom started the dishes. The Aunts returned to the martinis. Dad sat in the middle of the lawn, and I sat down with him. After a while, he lit a cigar.

Exposure

WHEN THE BIRDS started singing, Ellen incorporated them into her dream. She was in a large dining room with French doors at the far end opening onto an enormous backyard. Around a long table was a family that resembled her own, but somehow was not. The children wanted to know if they would be allowed to keep the ship, a full-size schooner, that had sailed into the backyard, yet Ellen knew the real question was whether or not the husband, and he looked a lot like Paul, would continue to have an affair. She knew this in the dream.

Birds perched on the ship's riggings, chirping and singing to the people in the house, *Keep the ship, Keep the ship*. Surrounded by leafy trees in late-summer green, the ship was in full sail, white sheets billowing and snapping in the wind.

Inside the dream house, a beautiful woman began fussing with a flower arrangement on the table. The man who was almost Paul asked her to stop, but she kept on, kept rearranging the long fronds and cattails reaching straight up out of the vase and the flowers and vines cascading over its edge. Ellen had a dreadful feeling that this woman had been in the house a long time, and then someone told her, Ellen, that the woman's breasts were perfect.

The birds on the ship became louder and then, suddenly, Ellen was awake. It took her a moment to realize that the birds were not on a ship at all, but in the trees outside her window. With her eyes still closed, she put a hand to her breasts and tried to remember every detail of the dream, the arrangement of the room, the color of the flowers. She was quiet a few moments, breathing lightly, her stomach rising and falling against her nightgown. It was a cool spring, but she kept only a single blanket on the bed. She slept on her back and did not like too much weight pressing on her toes.

Ellen was not a writer who relied much on her dreams, but occasionally she found things of use in them. Twice she'd found characters and once the opening of a novella: *Julia's analyst told her that love, hate, and envy were the primary colors of emotion; everything else was mixed from them.* She had read interviews with writers who revealed that they wrote down their dreams every day as a way of getting into difficult material. Apparently they mined their dreams—Ellen sometimes pictured them wearing hard hats, yellow—believing that the best writing came from a place they did not have waking access to. This was not a process Ellen cared to know more about. She did not talk about writing that way.

With dawn came rain, a steady hush against the screens of her bedroom. She felt there was something in her dream she wanted to remember, but it eluded her. She listened to the birds moving about in the rain-soaked bushes near the house, a flutter of wings against wet leaves, some scattered drops on the windowsill. Every so often, she heard a few clipped notes. Was it a song born of impatience or sadness, she wondered? If the rain kept up, her front walk would be covered with half-drowned worms in a few hours. Perhaps the birds were singing in anticipation, she thought, and in that instant remembered what had been dancing around the edge of her consciousness. It was not from the dream. Pressing her palms to her stomach to ease the rising nausea, she opened her eyes. Today her photograph would be taken.

In the past six months, Ellen Renwick's latest novel had won several of the country's most prestigious prizes. First, the National Book Critics Circle Award in an excruciating ceremony in New York she attended with her editor. At the reception, she'd met her agent for the first time, although he'd been her agent for ten years, and while he gripped his sweating gin and tonic, she realized that all those fuzzy, disorienting conversations they'd had were not the fault of the phone lines from New York to Seattle. Then the PEN/ Faulkner, a ceremony in Washington, D.C., that had been surprisingly pleasant. She had not wanted to attend, but when she learned she must in order to receive the prize money, she had asked her son and daughter to accompany her. Her editor was again there, and her publicist, wearing a ridiculous red dress. The last was the National Book Award. This ceremony she had not attended, despite her publisher's best efforts: they would put her up in the Waldorf-Astoria, they would pay for an extra night, they would fly her first class. Somehow she managed to withstand the pressure. At the ceremony, her editor accepted the award and made a short speech on her behalf.

The real problem was not the awards, however; it was the publicity. She'd won her share of grants over the years, grants that brought in enough money so she only had to teach part-time, but never awards that brought with them recognition in the form of interviews and photographs. Suddenly reporters wanted to spend the day with her, wanted to walk on her beloved streets and beaches, setting the scene for intimate revelations about her life of writing. They wanted to visit the places in her stories, and when she accompanied them, they scribbled down her every word, breathless for aphorisms and deep insight. They pressed her with questions about what it had felt like, years and years of writing stories and novels, raising two children practically alone. When did she write? Did she have a particular schedule? So-and-so sharpened twelve pencils every morning. What did she do?

Ellen told her publicist on several occasions that she didn't want to do any more interviews, but the publicist kept calling, tireless, relentless, and in possession of a seemingly endless list of reasons why interviews were a good idea. The list was based on the concept of *good coverage*. Ellen understood theoretically what this meant, but whenever the phrase was used she couldn't help picturing a large cloak pulled over portions of the map. If the publicist told her that an interview with an NPR affiliate in Atlanta would give her good coverage in the Southeast, in her mind's eye Ellen saw Georgia, Alabama, South Carolina, and the Florida panhandle go dark. It made her uncomfortable, but somehow on the phone with the publicist she would find herself agreeing to more.

"So he'll call you at home tomorrow just before ten A.M. your time," the publicist had said just a few days ago, after Ellen's last ultimatum.

And Ellen repeated, "Ten A.M. my time," while trying to press the number ten into a piece of paper with her fingernail.

Ellen knew very little about her publicist. She thought she might be twenty-three or twenty-four and came from somewhere in New England. When she was asked what on earth had

possessed her to become a book publicist, she said, with a studied mixture of candor and enthusiasm, "Because I love the
world of books." She had a bright, happy voice unless she was
trying to be persuasive or sincere. Then she toned it down and
her vowels lengthened and her diction became more precise.
The effect was that of a faint accent, sort of faux British, Ellen
thought. The publicist Ellen had had before this one spoke the
same way, leading her to believe the affectation was endemic.

"The interview will be an hour," the publicist had said.

"An hour?" Ellen interrupted. "I thought it would be thirty
minutes."

"Well, he may not need the whole hour. You can tell him in
the beginning that you would like to limit the interview to thirty
minutes, but this is for *Tincture?* The Seattle magazine that just
gave you the prize? It'll be great local coverage. Why not see
how the conversation goes?"

Ellen sank back into the sofa; she knew how it would go.
Good or bad, she would talk too much and spend the week
replaying the interview in her head.

"He's going to tape the interview. Is that okay?" the publicist
asked. "You won't notice anything. Maybe a few clicks and
beeps over the phone. I just wanted you to know."

"Fine," Ellen said. She took a deep breath. "But this is hard
for me. It affects my writing."

"The taping?"

"No. The whole thing. The interview, answering questions . . ."

"Oh, Ellen, I know. But think of your books. Each piece like
this reaches so many potential new readers. And think of the
readers who already know your work. Now they want to know
about *you.*"

Ellen and the publicist had had this conversation more times than either cared to remember. In New York, Ellen was sure, the publicist was leaning forward on her desk, supporting the whole weight of her head with one palm. On the opposite coast, Ellen was nervously tearing at the piece of paper with the ghostly ten, wracking her mind for some new way to tell her publicist she didn't want to do any more interviews.

"But why should they know about me? Why isn't my writing enough?"

"Ellen, the business has changed. This is what writers do now. To support their work. You write your wonderful stories and novels and when the books are published, you send them into the world with publicity."

"I send my work into the world with all the energy I have. There's nothing left for publicity."

"But think about all the bookstores and the hundreds of new books released every month. Anything you can do to bring your book to the front will help it sell."

There was a pause; Ellen never thought of her books selling. She imagined them held, the pages turned. The publicist must have sensed this for she drew in her breath quickly and added, "I mean to bring it into the hands, into the *lives*, of new readers."

"Will they have to take a photograph?"

"I haven't heard anything. I don't think so."

Ellen closed her eyes in relief. Through the phone receiver, she heard the small sound of a siren wailing in New York. "There's an emergency," she said without thinking.

"Yes, I guess . . . wait, what?" the publicist said.

"I hear a siren."

"That? That's not an emergency. The president's in town and that's his motorcade."

"Oh," Ellen said. "I see."

After they hung up, Ellen leaned forward and cradled her forehead in her hands. Maybe if she'd been asked to do these things at the beginning of her career, she thought, when she was young and lovely; maybe if then, instead of sending her batches of news clips about her books, the edges already yellowing by the time they arrived, they had asked her to do this work of publicity, she could have done it easily, gracefully. But now—now Ellen imagined publicity as a titanic beast, cousin to Virgil's Rumor. Lowly and fawning at first, she couples with Fame and runs over the earth, her head high in the clouds, her hands microphones clobbering writers into bloody submission.

A day later, the publicist left a message on Ellen's machine. When Ellen returned from her walk and saw the red light blinking, she was almost certain it was her. Her calls, like sorrows, tended to come in bouts.

"I'm just heading out," she lied when she returned the call. "I have only a minute." But her publicist launched into a long list of upcoming events Ellen should consider attending. She listened silently and when it was over, the publicist cleared her throat.

"Ellen?" she said. "I have one more question. It's been a while since we've spoken about the *New York Times* photo, and I know I haven't convinced you yet that it's a fine picture. Good, even."

At the mention of the photograph, Ellen's pulse quickened. "I know you hate it," the publicist conceded.

"It nearly destroyed me."

"I know. But . . . "

"My eyes are half-closed."

"I understand your concern about your eyes, but it really looks like . . . "

"It looks like I'm crazy."

"It does *not* look like you're crazy. You were squinting into the sun."

"We were inside!"

"Well, the flash startled you . . ." There had not been a flash, but Ellen didn't have the energy to go through the details of that agonizing day.

"My point is," the publicist went on, "our best offense is a good defense. If I could send out a photo you *liked*, papers could use that instead. Which brings me to my question. Since it turns out *Tincture* does want to run a picture of you . . . "

"You told me they didn't!"

"The photographer called yesterday after we spoke."

"You should have said no."

"I *did* say no. I said absolutely not, we're not allowing any more photos."

Ellen was holding her breath. It seemed the publicist was, too. They'd reached a critical point and both were unsure of the next move. Finally, the publicist continued in a rush of words, and Ellen exhaled in a long slow sigh.

"But you see then I talked to her, her name's Jennifer Foster, and she was very nice, I think you'd like her, and she convinced me to at least ask you. When I told her that you didn't like to have your photograph taken, she was very intrigued and started thinking out loud about how she could take the picture to reflect your, um, concerns. She even asked for a copy of your book. Isn't that great? She wants to read your work before meeting you. She's sympathetic to your feelings and really wants to try this. But the decision is completely up to you. I told myself I would not, absolutely *not* push you into another photo that you don't want."

"That's kind. Thank you," Ellen said meekly. She knew this would not be the end of the conversation.

"But, Ellen? Will you just think about it? Because I think this would be a great way to get a good picture of you once and for all, something we could substitute for the *New York Times* photo."

After she hung up, Ellen had to lie down. She tried to tell herself that the publicist was well-meaning, that she was just doing her job. But it didn't matter; she couldn't forgive her. The *New York Times* photograph, which she'd been told had to be taken or they would not run the story—and the story had to run for the sake of good coverage—had been a disaster. In addition to the strange look of her eyes, her hair was matted to her forehead. The photographer, a young man whose pale, delicate nostrils flared every time he lowered his camera, had been so intent on getting his precious lighting just right, he didn't bother to tell her to fix her hair.

She had gone to the bathroom before he arrived, but to her dismay the publicist had come with her. They came out of the stalls at the same time and stood together at the sink counter washing their hands, the publicist talking endlessly about how fast this would be, how simple and painless. She used that word, *painless*, so lightly, Ellen would remember later. Ellen had dawdled at the sink, vigorously rubbing at an imaginary stain on her hand, hoping the publicist would leave and allow her a few moments alone with the mirror. It was impossible for her to look at herself, to lean forward into the mirror, to check for sleep in her eyes, to smooth her grizzled eyebrows, to rub some color into her cheeks and lick her lips when a young woman, who was attractive in that steely New York way, was standing by her side.

"My hands are cold. I'm just warming them," she said. In fact, the water had gotten too hot and she had to add cold, which made the water come out too forcefully. It splashed up on her chest.

"There are paper towels over the garbage," the publicist offered. She was done now and waiting by the door. "I know this photographer pretty well, you know. He photographed one of our other writers a few months ago. He's really good."

Ellen imagined that her publicist and the photographer were lovers. She could see them eating in fashionable restaurants, New York hot spots, spending more time looking at their own reflections in every shiny surface than at each other.

"That's nice," she said. "I'm almost ready." She simply couldn't let the publicist see her pinching her blanched cheeks. Please, please leave, she silently begged.

"I brought some cookies, in case you get hungry," the publicist said.

Ellen gave up. After a few furtive glances at herself while she dried her hands, she turned to the mirror. The fluorescent lights were horribly bright, but she leaned forward and used the moistened part of the brown paper towel to wipe under one eye and dab the tip of her nose. It was a desperate maneuver, and the cardboard smell of the rough paper reminded her of highway rest areas and hospitals. Unseemly, sickly places. She straightened and tossed the towel in the garbage.

"All set?" the publicist asked.

Despite everything that had followed: the so-called painless photographing session that had lasted over an hour; the photographer positioning her between a closed door and a bare wall so that the resulting photograph looked like she was in some kind of cell; the phone calls from friends after the picture was published asking about her health; despite all this, Ellen woke from her nap with the firm conviction to let this woman take her picture. She would get one good photo for her publisher and then she would tell them, Use it or nothing. She would never again submit to a photographer's lens. She would retreat, just as many male writers before her had done. She thought of the famous reclusive writers: Salinger, Pynchon, McPhee, to some extent DeLillo. Were there any women writers this reclusive? She couldn't think of a single one. Was it because she was a woman that she had not been allowed to say no to the photographers? Why did everyone have a right to a woman's face?

Jennifer Foster, the publicist had told her, would call her at home to arrange a time and place for the photographing. When the call came, the so-called Jennifer introduced herself as "Jenny" in a very young voice and Ellen was caught off-guard. Fortunately, she didn't have to say much because Jenny was passionately describing how honored she was to be taking her photograph. She said it was an embarrassment to all who cared about literature in their city that a writer in their midst had gone unrecognized for so long. Everyone was humiliated, Jenny said, that it took forty years and three major national awards before Seattle realized she should be honored.

Ellen cleared her throat. "Well, if it must be quantified, and I really don't understand why it must, it's closer to thirty. Thirty years would be more accurate."

So when *Tincture* decided to give Ellen a special arts achievement prize, Jenny continued, the Washington arts council, not to be outdone, checked old files and learned they had given Ellen several grants over the years. A few days ago they had voted to cosponsor the ceremony for the presentation of *Tincture*'s award, which was why *Tincture* was extending the piece about her and had added a photograph to its layout. Apparently, Jenny told her, the mayor would be giving a speech—possibly, Jenny had heard, present Ellen with the key to the city.

"I bet someone's scrambling to make it," Ellen said.

Jenny seemed to think this was a joke for her benefit and laughed long and hard. "Oh, that's wonderful," she repeated several times.

As her laughing slowly diminished, Ellen bowed her head. Why was this business full of such young women? Jenny was quieter now, telling Ellen in sober tones that the publicist had warned her about Ellen's feelings about photographs.

"I'm sure she told you I'm difficult," Ellen said matter-of-factly.

"Oh, no," Jenny protested. "Not at all. She just said you were shy."

Ellen doubted that the publicist could have limited herself to that, and as Jenny began to relate what she'd heard about *the New York Times* episode, Ellen imagined instead how her conversation with the publicist had gone. The publicist would have started with *shy* and *timid*. Then, as they warmed into each other's confidence, the publicist's voice would have stretched and swelled until she was sharing a blend of information and speculation, the two sliding over and around each other like snakes. "You have to understand, her feelings are extreme." And, "She has spent her whole life watching other people. She doesn't like the idea of someone watching her." Ellen clutched the phone cord. "She's very difficult," the publicist might have said. Then, lowering her voice, "She might be," a luxurious whisper, "*agoraphobic.*"

Ellen released the cord and tried to listen to Jenny. She was saying that she might be able to take the picture in a way that would reflect Ellen's—and here she seemed to choose her own word carefully—*modesty.* Maybe through a window. Or a screen door. She might shoot her in profile, or in a concealing hat.

They agreed to meet at the house by the water where Ellen had once lived. Ellen didn't want her own house photographed and the idea of a public place—a park or hotel lobby were Jenny's suggestions—made her very nervous, as it did when Jenny referred to the meeting as a *photo shoot.* Before Ellen could hang up, Jenny said she hoped she would take an inspired picture of her, a picture that might work its way into the public consciousness, or at least the literary public's. That was her goal. In the library, she said, she'd found a collection of photographs of writers, all of which had impressed her: Eudora Welty at her desk, chin defiantly raised to the typewriter; Walker Percy leaning back in bed, a crucifix above his head; E. B. White at a plain wooden bench, a window beside him revealing nothing but water, horizon, and sky.

"Do you know these pictures?" Jenny had asked.

"I'm afraid I don't," Ellen tried to say nicely. "You see, I don't like author photographs."

The day of the photographing, Ellen dressed herself carefully. Her dream about Paul and the flowers lingered in her thoughts and she couldn't eat or work. By late morning, the rain had stopped and she read in her back garden until it was time to leave. Then she drove to the house by the water and parked on the road at the base of the hill.

The little house was where Ellen had lived when she was writing many of her early stories, before Paul, before the children, before the publication of her first book. Now the place was owned by the Washington arts council and a secret committee nominated writers for short residencies. She saw it mentioned all the time in the acknowledgment pages of new books, and she had wondered if the writers who worked there now were sometimes bothered, as she had been, by the relentless surf. She wondered if the radiator that heated the single bedroom still hissed and if the bottom middle pane in the window by the desk still rattled in the wind. She had propped a book against it on bad mornings. She remembered that the main room had a fireplace that whistled on windy days. When she started a fire, gusts of wind blew the smoke back down the chimney and into the room. All of her sweaters had carried the smell of those fires for years. The wool ones wore it well; the fragrance of fire blending with the something that was ancient about wool. Sitting at the desk, the sweater smell rising around her, Ellen had thought about wind-blasted sheep on Scottish mountainsides. She imagined them and their Highland attendants standing straight in the wind, and she thanked them.

When she reached the back of the house, she looked through the window. Residencies were not awarded this time of year, so the house was unoccupied. Standing outside the back window, Ellen had a straight view through the bedroom into the living room and out the front window of the house. While she was imagining her desk back into its old place, a figure appeared outside the front window. The photographer, Ellen knew immediately, and even younger than she'd imagined. She was standing with her back to the house, her long blond hair actually glowing in the bright sun. Ellen stepped to one side and peered around the window frame. She felt foolish, but she wanted to watch her, with the length of the house between them, for just a few minutes before they met.

It was a dramatic afternoon of wind and sun and Jenny was throwing herself into it, leaning her head far back, her hair blowing behind her like so much gossamer. What if I'd approached from the front, Ellen thought. Wouldn't she have been embarrassed?

As if on cue, Jenny opened her eyes and turned toward the front window. Ellen thought Jenny would see her and so stepped forward and bravely waved, trying to make it look as though she had just this moment arrived at this spot. But then she saw Jenny lean forward, frown a bit, and reach a hand up to straighten her hair. The wind seemed to have wreaked havoc with her part and she was gently tugging long locks back into place. She reached into her bag and retrieved a lipstick. She leaned closer to the window to apply the color. Good God, Ellen said under her breath, stepping again out of view.

She tried to take a deep breath, but could not. This is ridiculous, she said out loud, and stepped back in front of the window. She knocked loudly on the glass and watched as Jenny's gaze seemed to go beyond her own reflection, through the length of the house, and finally identified Ellen waving outside the back window. She seemed flustered. The lipstick disappeared and then she did, leaving the front to meet Ellen at the side of the house.

They shook hands in the bright sun. Ellen said, "I thought from your voice on the phone that you were a brunette. And shorter."

Jenny seemed taken aback. She smiled timidly and tucked her hair behind one ear. "Oh, well, no. I've always had blond hair. I haven't always been tall, though. I really shot up when I was a teenager. My mom always said she wished it could have been my brother."

"She shouldn't have made him feel bad about his height," Ellen said. "However, it's too bad. Short men are insecure."

"Well," Jenny hesitated, looking down into her bag. "I picked up the key this morning." She held out a small silver key and Ellen stepped around her, aiming for the front of the house.

———

Waiting for Jenny to finish her preparations, amid the zipping and unzipping of bags, the setting out of lenses and lights, Ellen worried about her face. The muscles around her mouth were twitchy and nervous. There was a stiffness in her cheeks, and her upper lip kept catching on her dry front teeth. Her eyes were watery, sensitive. Her face seemed all at once to be a set of features in mutiny. She hid this from Jenny as best she could until she was asked, finally—hadn't it been hours?—to turn toward the camera.

While she sat in the chair Jenny positioned, she thought about the small black-and-white picture that would be the outcome of all this fuss, that would be made glossy and sent to magazines and newspapers all over the country. A postcard bearing her image for the sake of publicity. With every camera click she imagined the product: that one with her face turned, that one with a slight smile, that one looking straight into the lights.

Eventually, Jenny directed her to stand by an open window; she was going to go outside and take a picture looking in. Ellen had to admit she liked this idea. Leaning in the window frame, she felt a gust of wind against her face. It carried the sound of voices from the beach. Children, Ellen thought, and she could see that Jenny had heard them, too. They smiled at each other through the loose screen, sharing the idea of children playing. Ellen leaned forward then, smelling the weathered metal that held, in tiny squares, the summers past of wind and pollen, the pungent promise of rain.

The cold air of late afternoon chilled them both, and Ellen, in a giddy moment at the end of the photographing, invited Jenny for tea. She didn't like to have visitors, but her relief made her magnanimous, reckless. They drove back to Ellen's house in separate cars and were now sitting across from each other in her living room.

"Do you know why writers take photographs with their hands around their faces?" Jenny asked, using her hands to demonstrate several familiar poses. "I've seen so many like that. Do you know why it's so popular?"

"It has to do with how they work," Ellen said. "Have you ever watched people working in a library? They smell their hands and knead their lips. They rest their pinkies under their noses. They clasp their hands before their faces and let their thumbs duel over their mouths. Libraries are disgusting places if you spend any time watching the inhabitants." She was pouring the tea and noticed broken leaves in it. "I'm sorry about that," she said.

"The libraries?" Jenny asked.

"No, the tea leaves." She was breathing unevenly, but she tried to explain. "You see, they're working away at something in their minds and at the same time they're breathing in the smell of their clothes and skin. You can see them smelling. Smelling and thinking. They pull at their lips a while and then lean forward to rest their faces just under the nose between the thumb and forefinger." She put her teacup down and plucked at this dry stretch of skin on her right hand, showing Jenny.

"It has to do with the need for one's smell," she said.

Jenny sat still, her eyes wide. "Smell?"

"It reminds them they're alive. An olfactory memento mori."

Jenny avoided Ellen's eyes and reached for her cup. She lifted it quickly, took a messy sip, and when a dribble of tea ran down her chin, she scanned the table for a napkin. There were none. She wiped the tea away, delicately, with the palm of her hand and smiled at the saucer as she set the cup back down. "May I use the bathroom?" she asked sweetly.

Ellen listened for the door to close, then got up to fix a plate of cookies. She was alarming the girl, she thought. From the kitchen, she heard Jenny blow her nose loudly and flush the toilet twice. She hoped she wasn't crying.

When Jenny rejoined her in the living room, Ellen offered her the cookies, grateful to see no sign of tears. "Let me show you a different picture of me," she said. She returned with a large, unframed black-and-white photograph. It was printed on heavy paper, the corners bent and softened with age. She placed it on the coffee table facing Jenny.

"How old were you?" Jenny asked, picking it up. The portrait was of Ellen's head and shoulders, the lighting done so that her skin looked like alabaster, dark shadows falling all around her. Her eyebrows were drawn, just thin dark pencil lines, and her hair was swept off her forehead and arranged around her face in shining, precise curls.

"Oh, I don't remember. I'd like to use it for publicity, but my publishers don't think it's appropriate. They say they need something . . . I believe *contemporary* is the word they use."

"It's beautiful," Jenny said, carefully putting it back on the table between them. "People don't take photographs like that anymore. Did you mind having your picture taken then, I mean, the way it makes you uncomfortable now?"

Ellen looked down at the picture. "It's difficult to explain," she said. It seemed very quiet in the house and she wished briefly that she'd put on music. "If there were no author photographs, authors would have as many faces as they had readers and readers would have only the writing to tell them what they wanted to know. But in this age of publicity readers flip straight to the jacket flap or to the photograph in the magazine. This is the truth, they think, and they hold the picture up close, like this, to study it better. I've seen them in bookstores." Ellen was holding her hands near her face in the shape of a book. She dropped them to her lap and smiled at Jenny apologetically. "This must seem silly to you, so young and pretty."

Jenny leaned forward. "But a photograph *can* be an insight into character," she said, and her confident tone seemed to surprise her. She laughed nervously. "I mean, I think you're underestimating photography. A good photographer should be able to draw out a personality, not just freeze a moment in time. And a good photograph should stand the test of time just like any other work of art. That is stunning," she said, gesturing at the picture on the table, "but it feels one-dimensional. It doesn't reveal anything essential about you."

"Well," Ellen said, suddenly exhausted. Why were all the young women she knew so tedious?

"You know, I have a friend," she began slowly. "She's about

my age and we walk together sometimes. A few weeks ago she told me about a man she met recently at a party in San Francisco. She told me all about him: how handsome he was, how he looked at her, what they talked about. She doesn't know that I know him very well. His name's Paul and she's right, he's very handsome.

"Her point was, or rather, what she wanted me to appreciate, was that she could have started an affair. She's married, did I say? The only thing that kept her from jumping right in that night, apparently, was the inconvenience of his living in another city. You see, my friend believes she's beautiful.

"I wanted to correct her." Ellen spoke deliberately. "I wanted to say, 'No, you're wrong. You are not beautiful.'"

She paused. In her lap, she pressed her palms together. "But I didn't," she said finally. "I didn't."

Jenny looked puzzled and declined a second cup of tea, which Ellen offered after a moment but made no movement to pour. Then Jenny said she should be getting home, and Ellen walked her to the door.

———

In the days before the magazine came out, Ellen felt good and was sleeping well. She rose early, wrote in the mornings, and took long walks in the afternoons. She began a new story.

One afternoon that week, while resting on a park bench above the bay, she noticed that everyone walking on the path before her passed through the same bar of sunlight falling between two cedars. All the faces were shrouded in shadow until they entered the slanting beam and then each person was illuminated for just a moment, everyone just the same. To Ellen, it looked like grace. She watched until the shadows lengthened and the sunbeam leveled out and paled. But it was still there on the path, a trace of warm light between the shadows.

Ellen smiled and felt that somehow this was a sign for her. She hadn't felt like herself since the publicity had started, pulling her into the spotlight where the givers of awards could make an object of her, a thing of fascination. People were looking at her again, scrutinizing her face, in a way she had forgotten. There was satisfaction in their eyes, but Ellen suspected it had nothing to do with her.

———————

"Jenny? Are you there? It's Ellen Renwick. I'd like to talk to you about the photograph. Are you there? Oh, God, I can't survive this again."

She hung up. She had heard her voice rising, felt her throat tightening, and she would not give her publisher an excuse to call this just another instance of her overreacting to a photograph. She sat quietly, leaning forward for breath, holding the receiver in both hands between her knees. On the floor across the room lay the magazine, crumpled and closed. Inside it was one of the pictures Jenny had taken from outside the house. Ellen had seen it only in a flash before hurling the glossy pages away from her. It was terrible——the writer Ellen Renwick peeking out from behind a screen, her face horribly broken into patches, scales almost, of sun and shadow. She lifted the receiver to her ear. She was ready to try again, but there was no dial tone. She held the button down until the skin under her nail turned white.

When Jenny's machine clicked on again, Ellen resumed, her

voice almost a whisper. "Quite simply, it's not me. It might be fine in terms of composition. Is that the word? I don't know much about photography, but I know this picture you've taken is awful. I can't even read the interview because I won't open the magazine again." Ellen was struggling to maintain control. She was afraid she sounded frantic, but she couldn't stop.

"It looks like someone who isn't well, or not right, hiding behind the window like that, the sun breaking across her face. Do you understand that I don't want people to see that when they read my books?"

She ran out of breath. When she tried to inhale she realized she was crying. "Publicity should have nothing to do with immortality," she cried. There was a beep. Ellen thought this might mean her message was cut off. Possibly it was a warning. She wiped her eyes and spoke quickly. "I'm afraid you're a nice girl with lots of equipment and no talent.

"I'm sorry," she added softly and put the receiver down.

———

In bed and sleepless, Ellen imagined Jenny calling the publicist, eager for any insight she might have. The publicist would console her. She would speak at length about how Ellen accepted bad reviews with such *aplomb*, so different from other writers, but that the photographs were impossible for her. Gradually the conversation would dwindle and stall.

Jenny, Ellen guessed, would save the messages and replay them many times. She would think about writing a letter. She might even consider stopping by to see Ellen, but with each passing week her understanding of what she might apologize for would diminish. She saw Jenny's life as if in fast forward, filled with parties and photo shoots, dinner out with friends, where she would begin the process of working the story into her life, choosing the dramatic and humorous details she would tell over and over again. A story that would feature her own patience, understate her own talent, and leave the listener wiping away tears of laughter at the idea of Ellen and her odd behavior. Eventually, the messages would be erased.

Ellen stayed in bed all the next morning. She wouldn't write for days now, not after this. She stared at the ceiling and remembered something she'd once read about the Englishman John Baird, one of the inventors of television. When he was ready to attempt the first-ever transatlantic transmission, he had hired an English actress and model, a *great beauty* as the papers of the day called her. He wanted her, Ellen knew, because he thought her beauty would make up for any imperfections in the transmission. But the night of the experiment, Baird couldn't make the equipment work. What did the great beauty do, Ellen wondered, while Baird and his team scurried about? Baird tried again the next night, without the actress and with fewer journalists after the stories of failure the night before, but this time everything was in working order. New York sat silent and waiting across the waves, while in London Baird was frantic for a face to send them. There was no great beauty in the room, only a journalist's wife, who, Ellen imagined, had come along out of curiosity.

Oh and they had to have a woman, Ellen knew, reaching up to cover her face with her hands. That part was historically and artistically ingrained. The image of woman always went first, cresting centuries of waves on thousands of ships' bows. So they pulled her out of the crowd and seated her in a chair under the hot bright lights. She sat there for hours while they refined this and that. Finally they got a signal from New York, and everyone in the London laboratory cheered. In New York, they had seen a woman's face appear out of the crude lines of silver static on a two-inch-square screen; the face of a plain woman three thousand miles away.

Did she smile, or did she not think of it, antediluvian as she was? Did she instinctively raise a hand to adjust her hair? Or was she tired and hot, squinting into the white lights? Ellen ached to ask her, the mother of all women who want to believe in the magic of their faces, what she felt at that moment.

The Trailing Spouse

T ESSA HAD BEEN LUCKY in love and because of it worried she would be unlucky in other ways. Her career, perhaps, or the conceiving of children. Temptation, maybe, would be severe with her. The health or longevity of her father; her mother had died when she was three. Throughout her twenties, while her friends dated with energy and abandon, Tessa spent many quiet nights at home with her husband, Nick. They'd met in college the first year and fell in love over the course of the following summer. After graduation they moved to New York, renting two apartments in the same building on the Upper East Side. The following spring they married and moved into the apartment that had been Nick's.

They were the first of their friends to start having dinner parties, two couples, two courses. Tessa could manage an appetizer or a dessert, but not both. Friends came over to their place and commented on the flatware, the everyday plates, the fancy china. "Is that a spoon rest?" they asked incredulously.

"From Florence," Tessa explained, a memento from their honeymoon.

After their fifth wedding anniversary and just before her twenty-ninth birthday, Tessa began to feel she needed a guide, a model. She was tired of being on the domestic cutting-edge.

While she cooked soups and nice pasta dishes and went to movies on weekends, her friends were still casting about, still telling wild stories of impetuous affairs and spontaneous trips. One friend thought she had a stalker. How could Tessa envy her this? She didn't, of course. It was something the stalker represented, some manner of living, she envied.

Sometimes Tessa wondered if the peaceful, supportive love she shared with Nick was imaginary. Her father was a mathematician, so she had a better-than-average understanding of odds—she couldn't be the only woman happy and in love. Perhaps she wasn't really happy, or not in love. In truth, how could she know? She hadn't had many boyfriends before Nick, and he was the first man she'd slept with. She felt at ease with him. He made her laugh. He worked hard at his job, was always patient and kind. Sometimes she would look at him across the dinner table or watch him walking away from her to work in his long blue raincoat, or watch him reading at night when he thought she was reading, too, and tears would come into her eyes. Surely this was love. She was lucky.

Over time, she worried less. This was after they'd moved to London for Nick's job with an investment bank and Tessa left hers at a quiet publishing magazine. It was a challenge, living abroad, and Tessa had other things to worry about. She roamed narrow streets, got lost in museums, fell asleep in cafés. Sometimes she went the whole day without using her voice, and when Nick came home in the evening it would crack when she greeted him.

"It's the damp air," he would say and urge her to lie down before dinner.

It was January and the first six weeks they lived in a small flat in Chelsea. They'd been told they had a view of the Thames, which Tessa had looked forward to, but they were on the ground floor and a busy road ran between their window and the water. It was unpleasant to watch so many cars whisking by. It made her feel the whole world was going somewhere while she sat still. She was the trailing spouse, the official term of the corporate relocation professionals, which evoked two images in her mind. In the first, Tessa saw a woman crawling across a desert, her thin arms straining forward, miles of sand to cross. In the second, on days when she was in a better mood, she pictured a caravan, camels and colorful tents, flowing robes. A well-organized entourage to a new land.

In the mornings, watching Nick dress for work, she admired his energy, the verve of the primary spouse. The leading spouse? She had asked the professionals, but they said there was no term. While he left every day at eight o'clock, it was all Tessa could do to put on her hat. She had nowhere to go, no one knew where she was, no one anywhere in London was expecting her.

In the beginning, she spent a lot of time watching the Thames from her vantage point inside the little flat behind the cars. Half the day it flowed to the right, filling up its banks with water that was often quite choppy. Then, at some mysterious moment she never quite managed to see, it began to flow the other way, smoothing out into glassy pools and eddies as it emptied into the sea sixty miles away. When the water was high, terns soared and swooped above it. They made the air seem warm and billowy even though she knew it was near freezing. When the water was low, the waders and shorebirds landed in flocks and scurried about the glistening mud. Occasionally a barge passed, but not often.

Some days she walked in Battersea Park, where, she was surprised to notice, the dogs didn't sniff her, an experience she'd never known. In Central Park it was difficult to avoid them. Was it her? Was it them? They seemed as reserved and well-mannered as their owners in wellies. She watched children playing soccer, stared at clumps of snowdrops blooming under bare trees. She could get a job on Nick's visa and had thought about freelancing for her old magazine, but Nick told her she had the gift of time. They were going to be in London only one or two years and his hours were going to be long. One of them, he said, should explore the city.

So she bought several books of London walks and planned long, elaborate outings that took her past places and houses of historical interest. She bought good leather walking shoes and a notebook that fit into the pocket of her coat. But it didn't work; she couldn't make it feel important to take a walk. If she retreated into a store or café, her voice identified her as an American. People smiled, but it wasn't something she felt like being friendly about.

In the spring, they rented their own place in South Kensington and their friends from America came to visit. Now, even without weddings, most of them owned flatware and china, so these things were no longer novel. Tessa served a proper English tea, mostly as a joke, but her friends took it seriously, thought it was fun, thought the crustless cucumber sandwiches were cute.

"I guess they are," Tessa said, staring at the cucumbers she'd frilled.

Although they were not married, her women friends wanted to talk about babies, and the men, although they were not happy or in love, wanted to talk about marriage. Both felt it was getting to be time. "How do you do it?" both asked.

Tessa and Nick smiled at each other as if they had many

secrets they didn't know how to share. But they did not. At least, Tessa felt she did not. She was glad Nick was not the kind of man who would make a joke. "Chocolate chip cookies," or something like that. "The key to every man's heart."

One evening in the middle of summer, Nick called to say he was going to be home late. They'd been in London six months and he was often late, but that night Tessa got upset. She brought a chair outside and began to wash the windows. Above her the sky was brilliant, the first clear evening in weeks. A mild breeze ruffled her hair. She looked at the windows, at the gray lines of dirt that traced the direction of the weather, right to left, across the house. All the other houses on the street were immaculate, several of them rented by other young couples. She started to cry.

An elderly woman came around the corner at the top of the street. She held a cane and had a bright silk handkerchief tied lightly over her hair. She was listing strongly to the left, but still making slow progress forward, like a sailboat tacking. She came up beside Tessa and stopped.

"It's a bit warmer now," she said. "The wind's down. That's what I hate. The wind around these corners."

Tessa nodded and watched the woman walk the length of the street. Then she climbed down from her chair.

In the fall, Tessa joined a support group for expatriate women. There she met trailing spouses of many nationalities: French, German, Swedish, Dutch. No women from Spain or Italy, though. She made a friend, Renée, another American trailing spouse, but louder and more confident than Tessa. She had a dramatic mouth, large and wobbly, and wore lipstick in deep shades of red.

Together, Tessa and Renée went to events organized by the club: jazz nights at the Victoria and Albert, lectures at the Royal Geographical Society. Many nights now Tessa was out as late as Nick. She asked Renée why there were no women in the club from southern Europe.

"More resourceful," she answered.

Renée had been a graphic designer in America. Her husband, Jerry, was a lawyer. "It's wonderful," she said. "Here, they're not reviled." Then, looking apologetically at Tessa, "Bankers are." She was not going to continue her work in London, however, because she was ready to start a family. They were trying, she told Tessa. For several weeks she would order sparkling water with her lunch, then one day ask for a bottle of wine. "It started today," she would say, shrugging. Something about the expat experience, Tessa thought, made them share intimate details sooner than they otherwise might have.

Through the club, Tessa and Nick began to meet more people, mostly American, mostly married. With these couples, conversation centered around relocation packages, rent subsidies, home leave. The cost of living, the cost of petrol, the inevitability of babies. How cultured and European they all felt, saying *petrol.* Everyone took long, expensive cab rides to long, expensive dinners. No one looked at the bills.

"It's important to stop converting," they said.

They seemed to know the rules of polite conversation, but not how to apply them artfully. If one of the husbands spoke uninterrupted for more than a few minutes, the corresponding wife would interject, "And how is *your* work going," addressing herself to another man in the group.

It seemed universal: All the husbands worked, all the wives were trailing. In the beginning, Tessa felt as if she'd gone back in time, except these women were not at home cooking and cleaning. They had housekeepers for these things. What did they do? Tessa wasn't sure until after she met Renée. With Renée's encouragement, she hired a housekeeper, too: Katia, a young Russian woman they found from a flier she slipped through their letterbox. They got many of these daily, but Katia's had been neater than most. When she came for an interview, she took her shoes off at the door even though Tessa wore hers. There was something soft and swollen about her face, as if she hadn't slept well or had been crying. Tessa found she couldn't not hire her and when she offered her the job at the end of the interview, Katia beamed, the rims of her eyes going red. "I think there must be no problem," she said.

With Katia, Tessa had more time than she'd ever known. She joined a gym with Renée and started seeing the women from the club daily. All of them, it seemed, had been given the gift of time. They exercised until their cheeks were rosy and their skin glowed. They shopped and discussed the best places to find rare American goods: chocolate chips, pumpkin-pie filling. For charity, they helped build a house and organized a clothing drive. For themselves, they formed a book group and planned trips and outings. They all agreed: they had time and money but it was hard. It was hard living in a foreign country.

Coming home from one of these excursions, a visit to Hampton Court Palace in September, the group was quiet, tired. They sat slumped in their seats, clutching their beautiful leather bags. The Tube rattled along and all of a sudden Tessa laughed out loud. The women turned.

"I'm sorry," she said. "I was just thinking. I was thinking

about the history of people who have had to leave their homes." The group was silent. "Refugees, economic immigrants, missionaries. We're so lucky."

There were furrowed brows, pained expressions of compassion. One woman clucked her tongue.

That night, washing her face before dinner, Tessa noticed the smell of cigarettes on her towel. She and Nick did not smoke, so she thought immediately of Katia, her round face, and pictured her smoking on their toilet, the cloud of smoke sinking into the towels opposite. She thought she could also detect a hint of the tea-rose perfume Katia wore.

Nick didn't notice the smoky towels, or at least said nothing about them, and Tessa decided not to say anything to Katia. She couldn't. She'd come home recently, exuberant from an afternoon in the city, to find her scrubbing the kitchen floor on her hands and knees. Tessa, horrified, bought a mop and a bucket, but the kitchen was small and Katia seemed to prefer her method. Tessa would run to the closet and hold out the mop, but Katia, kneeling, would focus somewhere halfway between the floor and Tessa's eyes. "I think there must be no problem," she would say.

She seemed close in age to Tessa and Nick, but they didn't know where she came from in Russia or how long she'd been in England. The only thing they knew about her, Tessa realized, was that her hair had once been light brown and was now dyed a dark red. At least this is what Tessa assumed, for she had light, exposed roots.

———

The second winter was long and dull. Tessa had forgotten that it got dark by three o'clock; it seemed impossible. Renée's husband was sent to Spain for two months, and she went with him. She considered waiting in London, but she was still trying to get pregnant.

Without Renée, Tessa began taking long walks in Hyde Park. She became intimate with the bird life. Why hadn't she noticed the birds before? They flew, they sang. What was not to like? She often took bread crusts and fed them by the Serpentine. The coots were her favorite, male and female indistinguishable, all black except for a thick white plate above the beak.

The club recommended creating an audio tape of cultural sounds as a creative way to experience living abroad. Tessa bought a miniature tape recorder and recorded the nipping of the coots, the honking of the geese, the sound of fourteen swans flying over the Round Pond in Kensington Gardens. In Holland Park one day, she recorded the lament of a male pea- cock as he sat high on a wall. The first forsythia was in bloom around him, yellow swarms among brown branches. Somewhere she'd learned that peacocks were kept by wealthy families in India because they warned of intruders. She searched for a way to describe this call, the haunting high wailing, but could not.

In March thousands of daffodils appeared, great swaths of yellow on the moist grass, and Renée wrote to say she was preg- nant. They would be staying another month in Spain. Tessa, alone in Hyde Park, watched the first bird families of spring emerge from the reedy banks and congratulated them.

One afternoon she tried talking to Katia. "We're really *both* expats," she said and asked her to sit down and have a cup of tea. She listed some of the things she disliked about London. "The way the women keep their purses on their shoulders while they eat. Have you noticed that? They look so nervous. And the way they say good-bye on the telephone? I always think they sound annoyed."

She thought as fellow expats they would find some common ground here. But while she talked, Katia kept looking back at the kitchen. She rubbed her bare arms briskly and held the hot tea close to her chest.

Tessa wondered if she was cold. She often wore a sleeveless shirt and jeans and seemed underdressed for the weather, but Tessa thought she wore these things just to do the cleaning. "Do you need to get back to something?" she asked.

Katia's face grew solemn. "No. I am happy here."

Tessa didn't know if she meant in England or having tea. She tugged uncomfortably at the generous neck of her cashmere sweater. "Will you be taking a holiday this summer?" she asked.

Katia shook her head.

———

In May, Tessa and Nick spent a weekend in Paris with Renée and Jerry. The weather was warm and bright, the trees had not yet filled in the long views of winter, and there was a softness to the air, a milkiness in the light, that made Tessa quiet and happy. Standing in line at a crêpe vendor's cart in the Tuileries one morning, Renée poked her. The men had wandered off somewhere and she pointed to the crêpe vendor.

He had beautiful hands, long tapered fingers and strong knuckles. They both watched as he swirled the batter around the pan and brushed on the warm, creamy fillings. He rolled each crêpe closed, tapped it—a stylistic flourish—then slid it gently into a soft paper cone. As he handed Tessa hers, he suddenly pulled his arm back and winked, first at her, then at Renée. He told them with his eyes that he had a better idea.

Tessa turned to Renée, who laughed and shrugged.

He would not give Tessa the crêpe she'd ordered unless she tilted her head back, opened her mouth, and allowed him to feed her one bite, the warm chocolate perhaps dribbling down her chin. He did not speak but gestured all this, touching his throat and chest. Then he winked again and laughed.

Tessa looked at his dark hair, his green eyes. The sunlight played over his face and she felt a pull low in her stomach. Her smile eased. Was this temptation? Or something like it?

Renée talked about it for the rest of the day, whenever they were alone. She described how Tessa had looked with her head tilted back, waiting. The chocolate had indeed dribbled down her chin and he had reached over to wipe it with his finger. She blushed when she remembered how she'd tasted the salt of his skin.

"I wouldn't tell Nick about your Frenchman, if I were you," Renée advised.

But Tessa had thought she would, sure that Nick would laugh at the scene, too. With Renée's warning, however, she lost her confidence. Renée had been pregnant two months and often seemed older, wiser. She had developed a pan-species view of motherhood and purported to know the thoughts of all mothers, whatever the genus. Later, when the four of them were walking in the Bois de Boulogne, she noticed a mother duck with her ducklings all in a row. "She's keeping her babies safe," she said, pointing them out to the group.

Nick smiled. Tessa said, "I know that."

"That's another thing," Renée said, turning to Jerry. "When the baby comes, we have to talk to Marta about the cleaning supplies. I don't want her using anything too strong."

"Good luck," Nick said, and Tessa looked at him. "Getting her to understand, I mean."

"It's hard," Jerry said.

"You wouldn't believe," Renée added. "The sheets?" She and Jerry looked at each other and groaned.

"You've never spoken with Katia," Tessa said to Nick.

"Of course I have."

"When?"

"Just the other day about the new quilt. She wanted to know if she could put it in the washer."

"What is it about linens?" Renée asked.

"But you're not at home when she comes," Tessa said.

"Neither are you. She calls me at work."

"She calls you at work? Why didn't you tell me?"

"It's not a big deal. I thought I could help," Nick said.

Tessa started to explain that she left the house on purpose because it was more comfortable for both of them, but the conversation had grown too personal and awkward. Renée and Jerry had fallen silent. They were walking ahead, holding hands.

When Katia started taking things from the house, Tessa was not really surprised. They had so much; she, obviously, so little. She started with kitchen goods—a bag of coffee, a bottle of wine—and it was easy for Tessa to pretend that they'd just been misplaced or finished without her noticing. Then, over time, a bowl, several wineglasses, a vase, a pair of candlesticks, and two tablecloths disappeared. Everything she took, Tessa thought, seemed necessary to establish a life in London, to set up an apartment and dine with friends. Tessa imagined the things in Katia's home, which she envisioned as sparsely furnished and cold. She pictured an iron-frame bed, a thin mattress, a shelf made out of crates and a board. What she saw, actually, was a room much like the one she'd had in college, her only reference for impoverished living. She didn't mind helping someone in such circumstances.

But when Tessa and Nick went away for a weekend a few months later and returned to a house stinking of cigarettes, Tessa felt betrayed. Nothing was missing, but several things were askew or out of place: the tea towel was draped over the kettle; the bath towels were not the ones out when they left; the sofa cushions were messy and misaligned. Nick also noticed several bottles of wine in the trash that he didn't remember drinking. The house, however, except for the smell, was clean. In fact, it seemed to have been freshly cleaned.

"What's going on?" Nick said when he saw Tessa's face. She explained that she'd thought of the arrangement as a kind of exchange.

Nick stared at her. "An exchange? What were you getting?"

Tessa was embarrassed. "A clean house. More time."

"But we were paying her for those things."

Tessa hesitated. "It's more complicated than that."

"I can't believe you told her we were going away."

"I'm not supposed to tell her that? Someone who comes into my house every week to clean?"

He said they had to retrieve the house key immediately. He didn't think it was safe for Katia to have it. "You're overreacting," Tessa said. "I think she just wanted to live in our house."

He drove slowly and with exaggerated care, as if demonstrating that the situation was under control. He signaled half a block before turns, he let pedestrians walk in front of them. It was a cool, windy day, threatening rain. Tessa sat very still, her knees together, hands in her lap. She stared at the last of the summer tulips, fading in bunches here and there. They always started the season so chaste, she thought, so upright and demure. By the end, though, they were an embarrassment. Bawdy and sodden, their petals flopped wide open for all the world to see.

"Nick," she said. "All that time you never noticed anything was missing."

He considered this. "I wasn't paying attention," he said.

They took Camden Hill Road out of the neat, flowery storefronts of Kensington and crossed into Notting Hill. They turned right on Ladbroke Grove and drove past several blocks of stately townhouses, the white facades gleaming in the stormy light. They crested the hill and ten minutes later, Nick stopped in front of a tower of council flats and left the car running.

The gray fifteen-story building was defaced by a colorful band of graffiti running around its base. Litter blew in small cyclones around the entrance and many windows were open despite the coming rain. On one side there was a slender tower connected to the main building by a system of walkways at each floor. It looked to Tessa like a retention area, a place for unruly occupants.

"The thing is," she said, "she's an expat, too, the real kind. We're the ones with no historical precedent. We could go anywhere and the corporate benefits would give us the same life. We don't even know what she does, Nick, besides clean our house."

The wind shook the idling car and he switched off the ignition.

"Renée and Jerry with their Marta," she said. "Everyone we know has a cleaning lady. When did that happen?"

She watched a gathering of people down the street, flattened by the wind, their trousers and raincoats pressed against their bottoms, their hair parted strangely against white scalps.

"Look," Nick said. "We're here, I think we should get the key. She's been a good lesson, and we'll do better from now on. Maybe we should go back to doing our own cleaning, but I don't want her to have our key. She could break in again."

Tessa nodded. "Yes. Let's do our own cleaning. I like that." The thought made her feel better. It seemed like the right thing to do. She turned to him, grateful, almost crying. He smiled and she leaned over and kissed him. Then she pressed back her tears and turned to open the door.

"No, you stay here," he said.

"What?"

"I want you to wait in the car."

"You don't want me to go up with you?"

"No."

"Why not?"

Nick looked up at the building. "Look at this place. I don't think it's safe."

"What about you?"

"I'll be fine, but I want you to stay here. Keep the doors locked." His voice was firm and Tessa hesitated. He got out and closed the door. As he walked away, he turned and pointed at her, a new gesture telling her to stay put. She watched his back disappear into the building, confused by his behavior and her own complacency.

He was gone a long time. Tessa learned later that it was because the elevator wasn't working and he was having trouble finding his way in the dim building. But that day, waiting in the car, she became desperate. She thought probably this was it, the disaster she had always expected. She imagined Nick beaten and bloodied. She saw herself running for a phone booth, riding with him in the ambulance, calling his parents overseas. In other scenarios, she imagined herself held hostage. She wondered what she would say, whether her captors would even speak English. When Nick finally came out of the building and thrust his arms aloft in triumph, the key dangling from one of his thumbs, Tessa forgave him the callous gesture. In truth, she barely noticed it, overwhelmed by a calm tide of relief and thanksgiving.

In America, Tessa's friends finally began to get married. Now they were grateful for all the years they'd spent dating because it left them assured, they insisted, that they had found the right mate. How could anyone take this step any sooner? they asked, forgetting Tessa and Nick, and Tessa and Nick smiled avuncularly. They flew back for all the weddings. They gave expensive presents of English wool and Italian lace. They were asked less often now for advice.

They took more and more short European holidays with Renée and Jerry: weekends in Nice and Barcelona, bank holidays on Lake Como. They talked less now about the pangs of relocation and more about Europe as their playground. In fact, they traded in European stereotypes. There was an unstated rule that this was acceptable as long as you said beforehand that this was, of course, unacceptable, that it was just a stereotype. But didn't it *seem* that Germans *really were* more officious and the Swiss completely unemotional and the Italians never busy.

The story of their Russian housekeeper became a colorful escapade, an amusing story that Nick and Tessa told at these gatherings and later, when they returned to the States. They told the story in tandem and developed an appealing mixture of humor and self-mockery. Nick had a funny part when he described the wine bottles in the trash bin; each time the number grew. Also: talking to Katia in the doorway of her flat. "You will make charges?" she kept asking. He hadn't understood her—*Make charges?* Was she talking about using a credit card?— but then he assured her that all he wanted was the house key. People shook their heads and smiled. How awful for you, they said. How difficult. Tessa, during the part of the story she told, often said, "Nick locked me in the car." Their friends shook their heads and winced. Such a dangerous neighborhood. They understood. The story ended with the fact that they had never hired another housekeeper; they managed without. This is what they said, what they told people, even after the reason in their minds became less clear.

When Tessa became pregnant, they moved back to the States; they felt it would be safer to have the baby there. They moved back to the Upper East Side, into the same building but a much larger apartment. Tessa faced morning sickness and repatriation issues, but she knew one would go away and for the other there was a support group.

Then, unpacking in New York one morning, Tessa found the tape she'd made of the birds in London. She remembered a watery afternoon when she had listened to the peacocks, those beautiful birds, and had tried to think of a way to describe their cry, the particular way it had pierced the damp winter air. She held the tiny tape recorder closer to her face. She breathed softly and leaned forward to better hear the sound. Several years and many miles away, it came to her: a rising note, more intake of air than exhalation. A cry as if the bird had suddenly recognized the wind.

Wreckers

Morning

JOHN BARLOWE and the woman sitting at the table across from him shared a surname, property in Ohio and North Carolina, two daughters. They'd been married thirty years and had withstood much disappointment. Occasionally, irrepressible happiness. John rubbed his hand across his eyes.

"You're misunderstanding me," his wife said again.

They had endured the deaths of parents, the divorces of friends. Once, the serious illness of their younger daughter. Turning to look out the window, he thought about the twenty summers they'd come to this house in Nags Head. They'd had countless meals at this table in the bay window overlooking the small yard, the stone wall at its edge with the little white gate leading to the sea beyond. Many years ago she'd given him the stone turtle that sat among the silk African violets on the windowsill. He loved that turtle, the way one of its forelegs was lifted in mute determination. He couldn't understand how the same woman could have made such a suggestion.

"It's just not a bunny, John. That's all I meant. Of course it has a right to live."

"I think it might be a mole, Elizabeth."

He peeked over the edge of the shoe box on the table between them and watched the stunned, fast-breathing, little gray ball. Her cat had caught it, the orange tomcat he hadn't wanted. Their first cat, Sibby, had been stumblingly aristocratic, a fluke of the gene pool, a farm cat with Siamese coloring. There was no kink in her tail, but she'd always held it very upright, showy, as if there were. She'd died two years ago, at the age of nineteen, and he still sometimes missed the weight of her on his shoulder. She'd balanced there effortlessly, and yet often couldn't make the leap to the kitchen counter on her first try. Now they had Hodge, the marmalade lump. How Hodge, this doorstop of a cat, had managed to transform himself into a hunter their first morning in North Carolina was a mystery to John.

Elizabeth moved her coffee cup away from the box. "What are you going to do?"

"I don't know."

They'd never brought Sibby to Nags Head. They'd always left her in the basement of their house in Cleveland and asked a friend or neighbor to take care of her. Like so many things, this had seemed acceptable before their daughters left home but was not acceptable now. Now the cat came with them. Now they owned two different cat carriers and drove twelve hours to their summer vacation with an open pan of cat litter in the trunk.

With his fork, he poked some holes in the cardboard lid.

"I don't think you have to do that," Elizabeth said. "I mean with a jar, yes. But a box isn't airtight."

"Okay."

He could tell from the way her eyes kept darting to the top of his forehead that something was wrong with his hair. He dutifully raised one hand to his head and smoothed the curls as best he could. Elizabeth sat up and raised her hand to her own head, showing him what to do. His hair was not as thick as it had been, but it was still mostly dark. Hers had gone completely gray.

He fit the lid over the box. He hoped the darkness might calm the wounded creature. There was no visible damage, but when Hodge had deposited the thing at Elizabeth's feet it hadn't run away. And when she jabbed at it with her slippered toe, it had remained where it was, hunkered down, its head turned slightly, breathing fast. The sight had made him sick, and he'd started up from the table.

"Don't poke at it like that," he'd shouted.

"What am I supposed to do? Touch it? It's probably infested with disease."

After locking Hodge in the room off the kitchen ("Don't yell at him," Elizabeth called, "It's his nature to hunt") he'd found the shoe box and scooped the thing up gently with a dustpan. He wouldn't have minded touching it, but thought Elizabeth would say something if he did.

"I'll take it outside," he said and rubbed his eyes again. "Will you get dressed?"

Elizabeth nodded without looking at him.

"Okay. That would be good." He took a last sip of cold coffee and pushed himself up. This slow, conditional voice he used with her now made him feel heavy, but she often spent the whole day in bed. He hadn't meant to make the situation into a bargain, his handling of the injured animal for her getting dressed, but the morning seemed to offer no other choice.

Outside, he stood on the gravel drive wondering if he possessed the ability to kill this thing that was suffering. He wanted to put it out of its misery. But how was he supposed to go about that? Crush it with a shovel? Hurl it against a tree? When he pictured himself doing any of these things, he felt faint. Then almost immediately he felt ridiculous. It was a mole, or possibly a baby mouse, he really wasn't sure. Either way, it seemed preposterous to allow the situation to derail his whole day, his first morning in his beloved Nags Head. He went back in the house and called the SPCA. Mole or mouse, it didn't matter; they couldn't take it. They were overburdened with family pets, the boy on the phone explained, cats and dogs abused and abandoned.

"What about rabbits?" John asked, staring at Elizabeth's empty chair. She'd left Hodge and the breakfast dishes and gone upstairs.

Yes, they took rabbits. And ferrets. They had two of these now. Also, as of this morning, one fox with a broken leg.

Standing in the kitchen, the phone pressed to his ear, John's mind reeled with the picture of so much wild misery. He could hear the chaos of this ailing animal world, the barking and caterwauling behind the voice on the phone. Above him, Elizabeth was running water for her bath. He had the uncomfortable feeling that he was doing something wrong, that there was a relatively simple solution to this problem that he just wasn't seeing.

The boy seemed to sense John's distress. He knew of someone, he said, who took in wild animals and healed them, if possible, before releasing them. He gave John her address.

John cleared the table and washed the dishes. He wiped down the sink, then started upstairs to tell Elizabeth where he was going. The woman lived far away and he would be some time. Halfway up, he stopped on the landing and stood with his head bowed. There was no noise now coming from the bathroom, which meant Elizabeth's bath was drawn. She was probably already soaking. If he talked to her through the door, she would ask him to come in. If he refused, she would get angry; if he obliged, he knew he would not be able to look at her body in the water with the love and desire she craved. He thought it best, right now, when they had only just arrived for their vacation, to spare them this spectacle of themselves. He went back downstairs and wrote a note in the kitchen.

Outside again, John felt light-headed. A wind was stirring, the air smelled of rain. This was his vacation and he wished for simplicity, another cup of coffee, the newspaper. He crouched and put the box on the ground. The motion relieved the tension in his back and for a moment he felt better. He lifted the lid. The gray ball was trembling. Its black eyes glistened, alert and aware.

Afternoon

It took a few days to open the house, a few more to close it up again. There was the drive, which John said was twelve hours but was really closer to fifteen. He liked to say they could leave at nine in the morning and be in Nags Head by nine at night, but in all the years they'd been making this drive, Elizabeth couldn't remember one in which they'd pulled into the driveway before midnight. John simply didn't think about the stops required for food, gas, bathrooms. All the effort hardly seemed worth it for a few weeks of sun and sand. But John loved the house, and Elizabeth, bathed now and wrapped in a fresh cotton robe, was surprised to find herself feeling fond of it, too.

She was lying on the bed, on top of the quilt she'd cleaned and stored at the end of last summer. For a moment, everything seemed all right. Her back was sore from the drive, but the bath had helped. There were two windows in the room and all that was visible to her was white and green: a white room, a white sky and, to the left, a bit of the willow that stood next to the house. Its long green tendrils swayed in the wind. From time to time a gust reached Elizabeth through the screens and she breathed the salty scent. She could hear the ocean, not a sound she craved as John did, but she found it soothing. John believed there was something about the sea, some atavistic need to be near water, that all people shared. Elizabeth used to smile when he said such things. Now she was likely to say she didn't feel that way and, in fact, had always preferred the mountains. These opinions generally made John uneasy and quiet, but after thirty years of wedlock during which she'd been the quiet one, the reversal thrilled her.

She looked around the room and remembered when the house had smelled of mildew and there weren't enough sheets and towels and the mattresses were old and lumpy. It had been left to John by his father, who, in his last years, his health failing, had let the place deteriorate. It required an enormous amount of work over many years, most of which, on the inside, fell to Elizabeth. John's work, at home and on vacation, was on the outside. He and the girls built the back patio, repaired the small sailboat, and turned the garage into a workroom, while Elizabeth thought about curtains, pillows, towels, sheets, quilts, blankets. She did not do this kind of thing naturally, keeping and decorating a summer house. She and John were not the kind of people who had ever had a summer house, or ever expected to have one. Other people managed these things simply; she heard stories from friends but could never quite gather the details.

She smoothed her hands over the quilt, the tiny stitches like braille beneath her fingers. The white cotton smelled pleasantly of rosemary and cedar, but her promise to John felt like a pool of cold water in her stomach. It should be easy to rise, dress, go downstairs, and yet she felt sluggish to the point of immobility, her physical strength as diminished as her will.

In the first years, John arrived at the house in high spirits, a camper's or a soldier's sense of mission and adventure carrying him through the work of settling in. The first morning, after their late-night arrival, he would refer to the girls as his troops and promise them a trip for ice cream in the afternoon if they got their assignments squared away. Accustomed to their quiet, work-weary father, this new commander delighted them. They giggled and played along, saluting him and running off to their tasks. Feeling slightly out of step, she would leave them to the house, the boat, the survey and repair of patio furniture and beach toys, and go to buy the groceries.

The girls came every summer when they were in college, but now they lived in New York and Boston. They had jobs that allowed them only two weeks' vacation a year and they didn't always manage to get to North Carolina. They came to Ohio for a week at Christmas. The second week they wanted to spend with friends, boyfriends. Elizabeth understood this; John struggled.

He had gone out, she thought. She didn't know where. Something to do with the animal, she hoped, whatever it was. A car turned up the road and she held her breath. When it passed, she exhaled. She longed for Hodge's warmth against her leg. He usually came running when she called, but the house was quiet.

This year John seemed to have arrived in Nags Head as tired as she. The drive was getting harder for him. All day she'd watched him shift uncomfortably in the driver's seat. The fact that neither of the girls was coming this year had him down. One night a few weeks ago, she'd said to him, "Don't you want to be there with just me?" and was surprised to sound more hurt than she felt.

"Of course," he said. "Of course. It's just different. Don't you feel that way?"

She did, but not as much. The girls brought out the best in their father. They had fun with him and he came alive around them; the three of them joked and teased and laughed. With her the atmosphere was solemn. The girls talked earnestly of self-improvement, vitamins, books, exercise. They brought her candles and special teas. It was exhausting, all the evidence that she was not living the way they wanted her to.

She called Hodge again. He had a quiet meow, more of a soft squeak that was at odds with his large body. She thought she might hear him downstairs, exploring the new place. She rolled over on her side and stared at the white wall. When her eyes closed, she didn't notice. She was full of sleep.

Evening

"Would you like a drink?" John shifted in the doorway. He heard the edge in his voice, and tried again.

"Can I make you a drink, Elizabeth?"

She was on the bed, her robe fallen open. Hodge, who had dashed upstairs when John finally released him, was curled against her bare stomach. Both of them were sound asleep, Hodge's paws twitching with his dreams. The room was hot; Elizabeth's hair damp and matted.

"Elizabeth," John said. She stirred and clutched at the cat. Hodge started and jumped off the bed. Elizabeth opened her eyes, slowly focused on John, and blinked.

"I'm going to have a drink," he said. "It's nearly seven o'clock. Would you like one."

"That would be nice." She sat up, pulling her robe closed

with one hand, lifting the hair from her forehead with the other.

"Gin and tonic?"

"Okay."

John turned and went downstairs. From a cool, stormy morning the afternoon had become bright and warm. The reversal had left him unsettled. If a clear day clouded over, he didn't mind; he often found it comforting. But when a stormy morning cleared he felt deceived, as if expectations had been raised without warning. In the kitchen, he filled two glasses with ice, pleased that he'd thought to fill the trays that morning. He listened to Elizabeth pattering about overhead.

When she came down, she was in a pale blue sundress, her hair brushed, a bit of pink on her lips. She walked into the kitchen and stopped.

John busied himself with the drinks. He could see that she'd made an effort, but he couldn't bring himself to say anything. "Do you want a lime?" he asked.

"Do we have any?" She looked around the kitchen. "No." She smoothed the dress around her waist and walked to the counter. She picked up John's note from the morning.

"Oh, I—" he said.

"You found someone to take the mole?"

"The SPCA recommended her."

"Did she think it would live?"

John poured the tonic into the glasses slowly, allowing the bubbles to settle as the liquid rose. "The mole died before I got there."

"Oh. What did you do with it?"

"I'm surprised you're interested," he said. They were both watching his pouring and he rested the top of the bottle on the lip of the glass.

"It's okay," he said. "I took care of it." He lifted the bottle and screwed the cap back on. "Shall we go out on the patio?"

Their backyard was a rectangle, a narrow lane to the sea. A small cement patio sat low against the house, two empty terracotta planters marking its far corners. Grass grew in the rest of the sandy yard, but not well.

They sat at an angle to each other: Elizabeth in a patch of shade from the willow, John in the warm late sunshine. It was high tide, but from the low patio they couldn't see the sand or the line of waves hitting the shore. Their view over the stone wall was farther, of still blue sea marked here and there by sailboats. The grinding wail of a Jet Ski came to them on the wind.

"I hate them," Elizabeth said quietly.

John nodded. Hodge pawed at the sliding screen door. "Don't you want to let him out?"

"Not yet. He has to get to know the place. Otherwise he might run away."

Hodge's claws were stuck in the soft screening. "He's going to ruin it," John said, sipping his drink. Several streets away, a car alarm went off with a sound like a hovering space ship. John looked up at the deep blue sky.

After a minute, Elizabeth stood. She pushed Hodge back and slid the inside glass door closed. "Someone's coming up the front walk," she said, looking through the house. "It's Max."

John lowered his face and rubbed his eyes. Max Lieber lived down the street. He was a year-round resident, their summer neighbor, and every year he tried too hard to make them feel welcome. He lived alone and seemed to have few friends. A couple of times John and Elizabeth had gone out for a drink at the Colony Inn and seen Max sitting alone. John felt sorry for him, but he came to North Carolina for a vacation, which to him meant an escape from social obligation.

Elizabeth glanced in John's direction, then drew back the glass door with a flourish. "Hi, Max!" she called. "We're around back." Hodge ran out. She tried to close the door on him and caught him around the middle for a moment. "Oh!" she cried, "John, help," but she released the pressure and Hodge squirmed through. He ran low to the ground across the yard and hunkered down by the back wall, his tail flicking back and forth.

"What do you want me to do, Elizabeth?"

"Nothing. Make Max a drink," she said under her breath, then turned to greet Max as he came through the side gate.

Max had a small round head on top of a long neck. The effect, as he sat telling them about his difficult year, twisting and turning in his seat, was serpent-like. The sun sank and they drank gin-and-tonics and Max told them his business was failing. He led boat tours along the coast for tourists hoping to see dolphins, but the sightings were getting rarer and the tourists were more interested in parasailing and Jet Skis. Elizabeth found some mixed nuts in the pantry and brought them out unceremoniously in the tin. While he talked, Max ate small handfuls, each time brushing the nut dust from his palms as if not intending to have any more. Slowly he was finishing the tin. John didn't like nuts, and Elizabeth took a small pile for herself and placed them on a napkin. She turned her chair slightly so that she could keep an eye on Hodge, who continued to slink along the inside of the wall beneath the dune grass.

"I'm sorry we don't have anything else to offer you, Max," Elizabeth said.

"Elizabeth," said John.

"Oh," Max started, chewing hurriedly, rubbing his hands vigorously on his legs.

"What? We arrived last night and haven't done the shopping." She looked at John.

"Max, can I get you another drink?" John asked.

"I'm sorry," he said, swallowing. "I forgot to eat lunch. But I've already got something in the oven for dinner. Would you like to join me? I've got enough, I think . . . "

"We couldn't. Another night," John said.

A lightning bug appeared and Hodge leapt toward it from his hiding place. He landed with a thud. "Not very graceful," Elizabeth called.

John held his breath, wondering if the maneuver had been a success. Hodge didn't move, and John's eyes searched the growing dark. After a moment the bug flashed again, to the right, higher, near the eaves of the house.

"You've never brought a cat before," Max said.

Elizabeth shook her head. "No. We used to leave her at home. A different cat. This is our second. Hodge."

Max was fond of cats, and he and Elizabeth began a lively discussion. John went inside to mix drinks.

Standing at the kitchen window, he watched them. He could see part of Max's face and the back of Elizabeth's head. He could barely hear Max's voice; Elizabeth's was quite loud. He looked at the perspiration on the back of her neck, the way her heavy bottom strained the patio chair's plastic weaving. He lifted his eyes and far up the beach saw the signal from one of the Outer Banks' lighthouses. There were several, but he didn't know their names. He'd read that the name Nags Head came from the locals, called wreckers, who, before the lighthouses, had tied lanterns to their horses and walked them up and down the beach. Sailors saw the bobbing lights and thought they were the lights of ships safely anchored. They steered toward them and went aground, easy targets for the scavengers.

When he rejoined them, Max was telling Elizabeth about a little girl he'd seen that day walking a cat on a leash. "She couldn't have been more than six or seven, and this was north, you know, just past Duck, about six in the morning. I slowed down, she seemed too little to be walking alone so early. I didn't want to scare her, but I thought maybe I'd ask if she was okay. The minute I stopped she looked over and said, 'It's my birthday.' That's all she said. She was wearing a party dress. It might have been too small for her, I don't know. The hem was high above her knees but they usually are, aren't they, when they're little girls? She had white socks and shiny white shoes. She seemed confident, so I said happy birthday and drove on. Then I passed the town and saw this one small house decorated strangely, with those plastic eggs that ladies' panty hose comes in hanging from a sapling, and Christmas bows stuck on the windows and front door."

Max sighed. "I don't know. Maybe I'm being gloomy, but I got the feeling something wasn't right. This little girl with her cat on a leash, those cheap decorations. It was so early in the morning."

John looked grave. He listened to Max and nodded.

"Why is it sad?" Elizabeth said suddenly. "A little girl up early on her birthday? She was excited. She wanted to dress up. Little girls love to dress up on their birthdays. Maybe she was having a party later."

Max was nodding. "Of course, you could be right. But there was something about the decorations. I thought she might have done them herself."

"And why announce to a stranger that it's your birthday?" John said.

"Because she's a little girl," said Elizabeth.

Max agreed. "But it was so early, and she was just wandering by herself."

"She had her cat."

The three of them fell quiet. Hodge dashed the length of the yard, and Max said, "I guess I just felt like she wanted someone to know it was her birthday."

John saw the obstinacy in Elizabeth's face, aided by alcohol, and knew that it was no use arguing. She would feel attacked if he continued to agree with Max and the night would not end well. But her denial of the sad scene bothered him. Of all people, he felt, she should be able to recognize sadness and its effects. Annoyance blossomed in his chest, and he leaned forward for some nuts. He shook them vigorously in his hand.

"John," Elizabeth said. "What are you thinking? Do you think the girl was sad?"

"Oh, I wouldn't presume to say."

"What does that mean?"

Max started to stand. "It's getting late. I . . . "

"No, Max. Sit down. John's going to tell us what he's thinking."

"Elizabeth."

"Aren't you, John?"

"I don't think so."

Max stood again, this time getting to full height. "I really do have to go, but thank you both. See you soon." He walked himself into the dark yard and disappeared around the side of the house.

Elizabeth went inside, and John ate the nuts in his hand, slowly and one at a time.

Night

"I'm sorry," she said.

John had made dinner, and despite her insistence that she was not hungry, she had devoured the soup and canned vegetables he'd warmed on the stove.

"I'm sorry," she said again. "Thank you for bringing Hodge in."

John nodded and ate in silence.

She considered how he'd become like a cat, preferring not to talk or be touched while he ate. She reached over and touched the back of his hand on the table. He froze. The other hand, the one holding the spoon, stopped in midair. They held this position a few moments. Outside, the wind was still and the surf steady on the beach.

"Yes?"

Elizabeth laughed and withdrew her hand. "Nothing. Just a test."

"I see," John said.

He finished his dinner, then cleared their plates, washed them in the sink, and began to sweep the kitchen floor. Elizabeth remained at the table. "Are you going to have coffee?" she asked.

"Not tonight."

"You always have coffee. I'll make it."

He smiled at the floor. "That would be a treat, but I don't feel like coffee tonight. It's too hot." He put the broom away and stood before her. She sat up straight.

"I'm going up," he said. "The doors are locked."

"Okay. Good night."

When he was at the foot of the stairs, she called to him. "John? Can I have a kiss?"

He turned back, one foot already on the bottom step. As he pivoted he stumbled; a feint, she believed, to indicate the awkwardness of what she was asking him to do. Still, he came. She lifted her face and he bowed down and kissed half her mouth.

For a time, she remained motionless at the table. Hodge had curled up on a chair in the living room, and she watched the peaceful rise and fall of his round back. Then, just as she stood to go upstairs, a bird started singing near the house. It was a sudden, surprising sound for that hour. Was the bird in danger? She glanced at Hodge, but he didn't stir.

Outside there was a bright moon and the air was fragrant and cool. She could just make out the bird's shape in the willow, but she didn't know what kind it was or why it was singing. The song was loud and piercing, complicated and wide-ranging. She looked around and wondered why it hadn't woken anyone else. Grabbing one of the tree's long boughs, she shook it hard. There was sudden silence, then she heard a quick flutter, as if the bird had flown to another perch within the tree. Elizabeth remained very still and after a few minutes the bird started singing again.

She walked around the house to the garage. She planned to get something to throw and disturb the bird, but when she saw the stepladder leaning against the back wall, she had an idea. The bird and the night air had banished her sleepiness. She felt clear-headed for the first time in weeks, and she thought she might try to stay up all night and meet John in the morning, already going, as it were. Beginnings were too difficult for them. Out in the yard, the stepladder would give her a commanding view of the beach and the sea; a fine perch for a night's vigil. She looked at her watch. Just a handful of hours before she could start a pot of coffee for him. He would wake up to the smell, a sign of a house in good order.

172 JESSICA FRANCIS KANE

Elizabeth began to pull the stepladder forward when she saw the shovel behind it, overturned on the floor, and on the back of the shovel a dark stain. She paused, even crouched and moved closer, then turned and finished dragging the ladder into the yard.

The Arnold Proof

> When it is impossible to find the exact solution of a question, it is natural to endeavor to approach to it as nearly as possible by neglecting quantities which embarrass the combinations, if it be foreseen that these quantities which have been neglected cannot, by reason of their small value, produce more than a trifling error in the result of the calculation.
>
> From "The Nature of Mathematics," Philip E. B. Jourdain,
> *The World of Mathematics* (Vol. 1, p. 40)

PROFESSOR ARNOLD'S Wednesday morning lecture on the history of mathematics was going well. Late in the fall term of his popular "Pythagoras to Poincaré," he was lecturing, as usual, without notes, a source of pride for Arnold and some jealousy among his colleagues. He was about to demonstrate a Poincaré Fuchsian function, one of those delicate equations he'd long admired, when his hand stopped on the blackboard and the x he had started to make trailed off into a squiggle.

The blackboard, washed just before class, was so black it did not appear to be reflecting light. The half x was bright white and while Arnold watched, a piece of excess chalk broke away and slid toward the floor. Later he would believe that it was something in this movement—the unfinished x, the sliding chalk—that induced what followed. For five years he'd been working on a proof of the Riemann Hypothesis, the most sought-after accomplishment in number theory. In the past few months, his efforts had reached an extraordinary intensity. He was close to what he hoped would be the culmination of his career, the announcement of the Arnold Proof. But as he stared at the unfinished x that morning, the work of several weeks coalesced suddenly in his mind and he began to sweat, an uncomfortable stickiness beginning under his arms. He glanced back at the Fuchsian and slashed again at the board. The x was complete, but his thoughts were in a muddle. He could not remember the function.

He lowered his hand and turned to the class. "I'm sorry," he said. "I don't seem to be feeling well." He looked at his students, at the sea of impassive faces, some of them startled now into expressions of confusion and concern. He smiled. He'd always been fond of teaching.

"I'll see you Friday," he said, ending his lecture an unprecedented twenty minutes early. The stillness continued a few moments, the class unsure how to respond.

When the last backpack was zipped and the door quietly closed, Arnold remained facing the empty hall. That he was even trying for the Riemann was known to only a small number of people, and his work of the past months he had kept in complete secrecy. He'd neglected food and sleep, had been practically living in the mathematics department with only occasional forays home. He was tired, he realized, and stepped forward to lean on the lectern.

His work on the Riemann began when Wiles announced his proof of Fermat's Last Theorem, simultaneously thrilling and disappointing scores of number theorists around the world. Arnold had been one of them. His graduate work at MIT had been in the same area as Wiles and he, too, had worked on Fermat's theorem. He'd believed he would be the one to get it and when Wiles did at forty it was a blow. Arnold was forty-one at the time. After the proof was published he had not tried, as so many others did, to confirm it. He had simply admitted defeat and confidently focused his prodigious attention on the Riemann Hypothesis. That was five years ago and he had made significant progress. Remembering this, he pushed himself up, rubbed the chalk off his thumb and index finger, and quickly left the room.

Arnold had known he would be a mathematician from the day in school when he'd first glimpsed the abstract power of numbers. On the locker-room wall he'd seen a bit of graffiti: 2 + 2 = 5 FOR LARGE VALUES OF 2. This simple equation, a mere joke to some, had had a profound effect on him. While changing into his gym clothes, he marveled at the truth it revealed: the number two could never be larger than itself. He began to wonder if equations could be applied to natural phenomena with the same degree of certainty. By the time he walked into the gym he had an idea that they could, and the insulation this offered from the vicissitudes of fortune and luck appealed to him. He already loved numbers, compulsively adding them on digital clocks wherever he saw them, counting the tiles in his bathroom, the number of steps to school. So, five minutes later, while once again failing to complete the chin-ups required to pass physical education, he decided to become a mathematician. He set about devising a plan that led ultimately to the completion of his Ph.D. in number theory at the age of twenty-two.

He returned to his office on the third floor of the mathematics department, where, amidst the clanging of radiators and the rattling of his windows on their sashes, he sat down at his desk. He stuck his arms into the gray cardigan draped over the back of his chair and buttoned it over his blue oxford shirt. He exchanged his lecture glasses for his reading ones—bifocals gave him nausea—and leaned forward to blow a bit of eraser dust off the blotter.

Arnold knew he was working against time. With very few exceptions all the major developments in mathematics had been achieved by mathematicians in their twenties and thirties, a few in their forties. What was it about forty? He had long disliked the number and felt it to be associated with tedious endurance and frustration: Moses was on Mount Sinai for forty days and forty nights; the Israelites wandered the desert for forty years. Hadn't Ali Baba had forty bandit-thieves? There was something wrong with forty.

And Arnold was forty-six.

On bad days he thought he could feel his memory and concentration—the mainstays of his mathematical talent—retreating, fading into the distance like tired, vanquished soldiers abandoning him in the twilight while he prayed for reinforcements. He compared his situation to the Alamo and it was small consolation that this noble deterioration was understood and accepted by all who endeavored in the field just as doomed heroism was understood by soldiers. But it was true; the concentration and mental strain took a hard and early toll. Euler went blind. Nash went mad. Arnold, frankly, was embarrassed to have lived so well.

He had not meant to. He'd always worked long hours, traveled rarely, maintained few friends. His first hero was Pythagoras, not only because he was the first pure mathematician but also for his ascetic philosophy of life. The young Arnold had posted the Golden Verses on his bedroom wall and every morning strengthened his memory through the Pythagorean method of recalling everything he'd said and done the day before in the correct order. He often dreamed about Pythagoras standing in the Gymnasium, looking for his first student. He chose a boy, a gifted athlete, and persuaded him to be trained in the disciplines of mathematics and geometry in exchange for food and all the necessaries of life. All is number, Pythagoras told the boy, and Arnold believed it. He never slept late, always worked on weekends, and in twenty years had taken few vacations, never willing to surrender his work to the ephemeral pleasures of relaxation. The greatest discoveries in mathematics had come from mathematicians working intensely, obsessively, often in isolation, until the enlightened moment when they saw deeply into a subject and the direction of the field was changed forever. Poincaré's discovery of the Fuchsian functions in the nineteenth century was Arnold's favorite such story, and he taught it to his classes every year. After a long period of furious work, Poincaré had had a trio of sudden illuminations: the first during a sleepless night after he'd had, contrary to his custom, strong black coffee; the second as he placed his foot on the step of a bus in Coutances; the third and final breakthrough as he walked along a bluff at the seaside, having retreated there in despair. At each place he had a profound insight characterized by brevity and immediate certainty. Poincaré would later say that the only thing left was to write out the results. Arnold had always believed the same thing would one day happen to him. He'd spent his career preparing.

He worked on loose sheets of white paper, keeping different sections of the calculation stacked neatly on his desk. Pulling his chair close, he backtracked through a few pages, then slowly began working forward through the problem. After a few minutes, he

lost his train of thought. He'd heard a buzzing in the room, as
though a bee had flown in and was caught in the folds of the
straight gray curtains that hung at either side of his windows.
A bee in November? It seemed too late, Arnold thought, frowning and looking about the room over the top of his glasses.
He'd seen them sluggish and dying in the cold as early as September, their bodies small yellow curls on the sidewalks.

After a time he was satisfied that it was not a bee and probably just the mysterious workings of the radiators. He scooted
his chair closer and backtracked again through the problem. He
was at nearly the same point when someone rapped on the
frosted glass panel of his door.

A noise he despised.

He shuddered and looked up just as his secretary, Georgette,
poked her head in. She cringed, a visual apology, for Arnold
had asked her many times to knock on the door frame, and
informed him that his wife was on the phone. Apparently, she'd
been trying to reach him for some time. Georgette and Arnold
both looked at Arnold's phone, then trailed the cord to the wall
where it was unplugged.

"Shall I transfer her?" Georgette asked, stepping quickly to
reconnect the line.

"Certainly," Arnold said, rising abruptly and unsteadily,
nearly tipping his chair.

"It was unplugged," he explained when Georgette put Mary
through. "You know I'm trying to avoid interruptions."

"How long can you keep this up, Arnold? You can't work in
a vacuum." She added more softly, "Doesn't nature abhor a vacuum?" and Arnold recognized the waning of her resolve. He
could hear the clicking of the gas burner, a sound as familiar to
him as the ticking of the radiators in his office. Mary, a smoker

for almost as long as he'd known her, was lighting a cigarette at the stove in their kitchen.

"Mary, I'm familiar with the laws of nature, but—"

"Are you?"

"Am I what?"

"Familiar with the laws of nature? Sometimes I'm not so sure." He heard a sob and then another click.

"Mary?"

Arnold took off his glasses and leaned forward. He massaged his temples in slow, small circles. These calls were increasing in frequency, but he had not yet determined their cause. Mary calling him by his last name, however, was a new variable. When had that started?

He put his glasses back on and looked at his papers. Leonhard Euler had introduced the zeta function, a power series, in 1740 and proved it was convergent for all real numbers greater than one. In 1859, the German mathematician Bernhard Riemann was the first to treat the zeta function as a function of a complex variable z. If Arnold spoke about his work with his colleagues in the humanities, a thing he did seldom, he had to remind most of them about complex numbers and their two components: one real, one imaginary. Their brows furrowed and he felt sorry for them. It seemed many of them had not studied math beyond high school and would never comprehend the exquisite beauty of a Riemann zeta function, as the zeta function with a complex variable came to be known. Riemann conjectured that all the zeros of the function between zero and one—called nontrivial zeros—fell along the line where the real part of z equaled ½. He was not able to prove it, however, and the conjecture passed into future generations as the Riemann Hypothesis. It didn't have the popular appeal of Fermat's theorem because it lacked the romantic story of midnight marginalia, but it was now nearly 150 years old despite the best work of Riemann, Hardy, Hadamard and others. For the beauty of mathematics, all number theorists felt, a solution must be found.

Arnold sharpened his pencil and attempted to sink into his work, to achieve that state of concentration he likened to suspended animation. If he could get there, he could work for hours, oblivious to the passage of time. He would not be aware of any part of his surroundings, not even of his hand moving across the page. After a minute, he shifted in his chair and scratched the back of his hand. Then he felt an itch on his back, just beneath his right shoulder blade. He used the end of his pencil to get it, then sat forward and held himself very still. A few minutes later, he put his pencil down.

He rarely left the mathematics department during the day, but now Arnold decided unusual measures were required. On the way out, he stopped to speak to Georgette. She turned from her computer when he walked into her office. "I hope I didn't disturb you just now. I didn't think you'd be in."

"Not at all," Arnold replied. "I ended my lecture early." He sorted his mail quickly.

"Don't you feel well?" Georgette asked, her eyes wide with concern.

He looked at her, at the small anxious face emerging from a cranberry turtleneck. The color of the sweater seemed to be reflected in two well-defined patches on her pale cheeks. She was quite pretty, he thought, and swallowed.

"I feel fine," he said. "In fact, I'm going out."

Exchanging the warm, somnolent air of the mathematics department for a brisk November wind was not as invigorating as Arnold had hoped, and he began to feel uneasy. With each long stride, his pant leg rode up and flapped about his ankle revealing a tight brown sock. His shoes—brown leather, tightly laced—were dark and polished. He always wore the same kind and noted the changing styles on campus with a certain academic interest. Currently, he believed, shoes of all kinds were being worn without socks. How cold that must be, he thought.

He headed across the green. Students passed him on either side and he had the brief sensation that he was going the wrong way. He was buffeted by bags and backpacks, swinging hands brushed his sleeves. He kept on, however, head down and fierce—like a salmon going to spawn, he imagined—and soon the walk and the wind had the desired effect and his thoughts began to clear.

There was a time when he had hoped for a position at MIT or perhaps Princeton, but the mathematics department at his university was highly regarded. Currently he was supervising only one graduate student, which gave him all the time he needed for his work on the Riemann. He'd had more students in the past, but he believed this streamlined state was better for his concentration. He had done solid work in several areas and published numerous articles in respected journals of mathematics and number theory. In addition, he'd written informal essays for several popular magazines on the lives of the great mathematicians, his favorites: Pythagoras, Archimedes, Poincaré. Also Gauss, who had corrected his father's bricklaying accounts at three. And Newton, who'd jumped into the wind on the plains near Grantham, measured his distance and calculated the wind's speed. Arnold had always been fascinated by these boys of genius, men of penetrating insight, and he hoped the story might one day be told of his own youthful number-intoxication.

At the corner of Elm and Church, he narrowly avoided a

collision with a reckless bicyclist. His beige wool pants were splashed with muddy water, the droplets fanning out in even intervals. He stopped and plucked his pant leg at the knee, twisting it around so he could better see the pattern, which, he knew, corresponded to the motion of the spinning wheel.

Such things interested him.

As Arnold looked at the muddy spots, an image of Mary came to mind: tall, slender, with gray eyes that still made him catch his breath when she looked at him with kindness, an event that seemed increasingly rare. He dropped his pant leg and stepped off the curb.

There was no denying it, he thought sadly. Mary was a beautiful woman aging well while he seemed to be growing shorter and rounder. He nervously caressed his stomach. They had always kept a good diet and tried to get a reasonable amount of exercise, but Mary, in recent years, had started to care more about her weight and appearance. She had not been able to quit smoking, but she'd joined a gym, a volunteer organization at the hospital, and three different reading groups—one, Arnold believed, devoted entirely to self-help. "Due measure in all things," Arnold believed, one of Pythagoras's Golden Verses, but Mary's physical and mental regime was formidable and had surpassed any boundary long ago. She was busy, rarely made dinner anymore, and was always exercised, brushed, and polished when he came home from work feeling limp, worn, and smelling vaguely of the strong cleaning agents used by university maintenance. What was it she was seeking? He'd asked her once recently and received an elusive answer.

"It's not so much seeking as recovering."

Recovering?

"I'm warning you," she said, and Arnold knew better than to

push. Never take a set of variables beyond their defined limits. Not Pythagoras, but good math nevertheless.

They had met in graduate school, where Mary was working on her master's in English and Arnold was in the last year of his Ph.D. From the beginning Arnold had been in awe that a woman of such beauty was attracted to him. He was not unattractive but he was shy and possessed no outstanding features besides, perhaps, an inclination toward tenderness. What was it she saw in him? He'd asked himself many times and thought he knew a couple of things.

This: The way when he talked to her about mathematics, describing his belief that it was the fulfillment of the passion for perfection, his eyes would redden with emotion and his hands would gesture delicately, as though shaping clay models in the air. Mary's eyes would glisten, her legs grow restless.

And this: The fact that his choking passion for mathematics had shattered his belief in words, his faith in language forsaken for the greater possibilities of abstraction. As a student of English, Mary saw this as a challenge and, quite imaginatively, a physical advantage. They'd shared a passionate youth.

They spent their honeymoon driving to his postdoc position at the university, the same place he'd ultimately received tenure. Mary worked for several years teaching composition, but when their son was born she left. It had only been two years since their son left for college; two years since Mary embraced a lifestyle that had nothing to do with the person she'd been for twenty-five years; five years since the Wiles proof. The numbers swirled in his head: two, two, five, twenty-five. There must be a pattern. These were the data, but where was the rule?

And yet sometimes Arnold saw evidence of the old Mary, or at least fissures in the new facade. She could dismiss him angrily one minute but ask for a hug the next. She planned elaborate outings with their friends, apple-picking excursions and museum visits, but then seemed relieved when he couldn't go. She spoke frequently of her low self-esteem, but would argue vociferously with him on subjects she knew little about, such as how the university should be treating him. She had long believed he was underappreciated. She was like a warrior with a new, unwieldy weapon. Proclaiming her new self-improvement theories, she stumbled sometimes and stopped midsentence, confounded by a technicality. She wanted to "reinterpret" their marriage, she said, and alternated between taking this concept very seriously, leaving Arnold quiet and wary, and poking fun at it so that both she and Arnold would laugh.

It was at these times that Arnold believed she was still a two to his three—the Pythagorean definition of the feminine and masculine principles. Together they equaled five, the definition of marriage. He'd told her this recently, had tried to share the beauty of Pythagoras's belief that numbers represented abstract notions such as male and female, love and marriage, opportunity and justice.

Unfortunately, she was watering the garden and remained unmoved.

"Are you trying to be romantic?" she said, narrowing her eyes at him and turning heedlessly in his direction with the hose. "Don't talk to me about that man."

He'd had to jump to avoid the parabola of water. The sudden motion prompted a thought about the Riemann and for a brief moment his heart soared. He thought he'd had an insight into the problem, but by the time he landed and began rubbing his twisted ankle he realized he was mistaken.

Thinking about the Riemann brought a tingling to his fingertips.

Or was that the cold? He'd forgotten his gloves.

Turning left on Vine, Arnold passed a sparkling store window. Out of the corner of his eye he caught his reflection and stopped in surprise. Was it the angle of light that made his eyebrows seem arched in such an expression of worry? He hadn't felt them up there, but as he studied this pale, semitransparent man superimposed over a travel agency's beach scene, the muscles in his forehead relaxed. It felt as if folds and folds of skin would descend over his eyes.

He blinked and stood taller.

Mary often stopped like this, he thought, in front of store windows. It was not really window-shopping, for she usually marched in and bought whatever she saw that she wanted. But she had not always been that way. When they were first married and did not have much money, they'd taken a vacation they could barely afford—where had it been? Florida?—and were walking along a street of shops and restaurants, like this one, but filled with a clear rosy light. She'd held his hand and pulled him gently to a stop in front of a jewelry display. A malachite necklace had caught her eye. They went inside but agreed it was too expensive. The day before they left, Arnold went back to buy it as a surprise but was again put off by the price. He decided on a pair of less expensive earrings. That night he gave them to her as they ate dinner on a terrace overlooking the sea.

Or was it the Gulf of Mexico?

"They're coral," he said when she opened them in the moonlight and he explained how economically they were a better memento of the trip.

"Of course. Earrings," Mary said.

Arnold tried to remember the last time she'd worn them. He couldn't, and after a few minutes he pulled his coat close about his neck and turned away from the window.

Several stores down, he stepped into a café. He ordered a black coffee and a sullen girl with a nose ring handed him a mug that was nearly overflowing. He had to lean over and sip it before walking to a stool by the window.

When had the students started piercing their noses, he wondered. Going around without socks, behaving belligerently? A young couple sat down to his left. They huddled close and began to kiss. Arnold planned to move, but instead just shifted a bit to the right. He tucked both his heels onto one of the high rungs of the stool and brought his bony knees together. Perched in this way he felt small, vulnerable. He sipped his coffee and listened to them kissing, to the warm wet smacking of it all. Staring out the window at the blustery day he realized he was very cold.

———

The problem with ending class early, Arnold knew, was that word would spread. That afternoon, with half an hour left in a small lecture on advanced number theory, Arnold decided to extend class by ten minutes in order to put an end to any rumors of his failing stamina. As he was considering what material to cover, however, he faltered again.

Georgette glanced nervously at the wall clock when he walked into her office. He was still holding his chalk.

"Yes, yes," he said, avoiding her eyes. "I finished early." As there seemed to be nowhere else to put it, he handed her the chalk and walked out.

Standing by his windows, Arnold wondered if he should go out again. It was the time of day when the students roamed the campus luxuriously, with a sense, amidst all their young worries, that life would never be like this again. It was a thing they understood vaguely, Arnold thought, and yet were absolutely correct. The clouds had dispersed and a few students sat on a bench in a patch of sun. Two girls pulled up their skirts, exposing pale, naked legs well past the knee to the wan sunlight and the entirety of the mathematics department.

Arnold squinted to see them better. November and no tights or stockings? Or were those stockings he just couldn't see, pale or buff or nude? He leaned quickly toward the window and bumped his forehead against the glass. He jerked back and reached up to rub the spot. But they wouldn't expose their legs to the sun if they didn't hope to get tan, he thought, and didn't they know that ultraviolet rays wouldn't penetrate nylon?

He was leaning again, slowly, toward the window when he noticed someone he knew on the steps of the library, Patrick MacDonald, professor of physical chemistry. Arnold liked him; they had been seated next to each other at several university events. It looked as if he were watching the same group of girls, but then he glanced up suddenly in the direction of Arnold's window. Forgetting the distance between them, Arnold called his name and waved. MacDonald stood and walked away.

Arnold dropped his hand and looked again at the green. The girls were gone, but his attention was caught by a different spectacle. It was a sad truth that an aging mathematician's mental decline did not necessarily correspond to his physical vitality. In the worst cases, the relationship was quite appallingly inverse. Thus the humiliating daily sight of the senior mathematicians leaving the department in small groups in the midafternoon, their new gym bags bouncing against their pale legs, the creases from their work socks still visible on their skinny calves. There was Sackler, Gutman, Fish—their combined work had revolutionized probability theory fifteen years ago. Now they were learning handball, racquetball, tennis. Arnold wondered if he would one day join them.

The phone rang and he turned from the window. "Look, Arnold," Mary said. "I'd like to talk to you." Her voice wavered but remained strong. "Can I come down there?"

Arnold walked around his desk, the phone pressed tightly to his ear. As he sat down, he glanced desperately outside. The cold wind still gusted, rattling his windows in their frames, and in his office the radiators began again their syncopated ticking. Such a hollow, melancholy sound, he thought, and yet the constant companion to his work.

"Hello?" Mary said. "What are you doing?"

"Nothing."

"I don't believe you. What is it? The Riemann? How's it going?"

"I can't really explain."

"You mean you don't want to."

"No. It's more complicated. I . . ." he stopped.

"What's wrong? Is language failing you?"

"No, I mean . . . Yes." It seemed to Arnold that increasingly he was having difficulty communicating. Maybe language *was* failing him. He heard the burner clicking and realized Mary was lighting another cigarette.

"Why are you calling me Arnold?" he asked suddenly.

"It's an abstraction. You of all people should understand that."

He was silent.

"Oh, dear," she said.

He began breathing and counting silently to ten, an old habit, each number on the exhale. In Pythagorean cosmology, breath and number were related. He had always found that reassuring.

At two, Arnold thought he would ask Mary if she remembered where that vacation had been, and if she still had those earrings.

"Arnold?" Mary said softly. "A rolling stone gathers no moss." She'd often said this about his counting. It was an old joke between them, and she said it now with tenderness. At five, he thought the expression was more useful than it seemed. He wished he'd heeded it long ago.

At eight, he recognized the value of her wanting to understand his work. She'd always urged him to tell her about it, but since he began on the Riemann he'd done so less and less.

At ten, Arnold took a deep breath and found his voice. Before he could use it, however, Mary spoke again. "I'm so worried," she said. "What will you have if we both leave you?"

"Who?"

"Mathematics," she said quietly. "And me."

The wind died down and a late afternoon stillness settled over the university. The clouds moved together imperceptibly until the sky was a somber field of gray. Students hurried home from late classes; the dining halls started dinner, sending warm vegetable smells into the cold air. Overhead, sparrows came together in soaring assembly and here and there grackles pierced the air with their prehistoric cries.

In his office, Arnold sat motionless at his desk, unaware of these end-of-day goings-on. He'd reassured Mary for the time being, though he couldn't remember exactly how. All he knew for certain was that she wasn't coming in to campus and that they were going to talk more that night. After they hung up, he'd tried to return to the Riemann, but now and then he thought about her and the night ahead and it distracted him. She'd said something on the phone, something he could only grasp in his memory for a moment before it faded. It would stay just long enough to make him uneasy, then disappear.

He looked down at his papers, then leaned over to smell their lamp-warmed sweetness. If he could smell the work, he thought, smell the pages, then all the nontrivial zeros might behave. But mathematics is logical, not psychological in nature, he reminded himself, and his head, low to the desk, began to nod. As he dozed off, he saw Archimedes struck down by a Roman soldier while he was measuring a figure in the sand.

———————

Two hours later, Arnold was sitting in his car in the parking garage. He was late, which meant Mary would be waiting for him in the shadowy half-dark of the kitchen, lighting her cigarettes in the stove's dull purple flame. Their house was just a few miles from campus near the perimeter of town. If he took his regular route, he would be home in fifteen minutes. He gripped the top of the steering wheel. But he wouldn't, he decided. He would take Grove Avenue to the other side of town and from there get the interstate home. It was a giant loop that would take nearly three times as long, but he would be out in the country. The open road, he thought, starting the car, would help him clear his mind.

He'd been on the highway about ten minutes when he pulled

into a rest area to get a cup of coffee. As he got out of the car, he could feel his mouth smiling broadly, compulsively. He stretched his jaws into a yawn and rubbed his cheeks, but the smile returned. It was uncomfortable. The coffee was easy to buy, just a matter of pushing the correct sequence of buttons on a vending machine. Clutching his cup, Arnold thought about the rest area, how it was like an escape from the effects of entropy, a momentary halting of the disintegration. Didn't hungry people come to be filled, tired people to rest? All the things that wore one down—stress, hunger, fatigue—were rectified here.

He liked the idea. The rest area as a place of equilibrium. He would not rush away.

Instead of heading back to his car, Arnold wandered over to the edge of the parking lot. The whole place was built over the highway, and he leaned over the cement balustrade and looked down. A group of cars passed beneath him, then a few stragglers, then another group; an example of wave theory. He stood and noticed someone against the balustrade farther down.

"Hello," the man said without turning.

"Oh, I didn't recognize you." It was MacDonald. "How strange. I never come here. Do you . . . often?" Arnold stopped. The question seemed foolish. "I saw you earlier today," he tried. "I waved."

MacDonald nodded but still did not turn. Instead he took a sip of his coffee. Arnold leaned again over the railing. After a minute, MacDonald unfolded himself—he was a tall man—and took a few lumbering steps toward him. "I'm sorry. I'm not myself today. I've had some bad news."

"I'm sorry to hear it."

"I've been asked to be an associate dean of the college."

"Isn't that good news? Congratulations."

"I don't think it's something to be congratulated about. I'm fifty-eight. The term is four years. When I'm done I'll be sixty-two, almost certainly with no grants."

Arnold considered this. "Can you say no?"

"Not really. They've picked me because of that prize I won a couple of years ago. When the Dean told me about the nomination, she talked about the responsibility of prestige."

Arnold remembered that MacDonald had been celebrated for his research. It had made a popular story at the time because he'd been pursuing one thing when an error led him to discover something else.

"You'll go back to teaching," he said.

MacDonald looked at him. "There are plenty of younger guys who can do the teaching. The last guy in this position spent a year in the library after his term was up trying to reconnect with his field. Then he retired, early." MacDonald looked down. "To answer your question, I stopped here because I needed time to think about the good aspects of the job to tell my wife. She's going to worry about me."

MacDonald gazed out over the road, and Arnold studied his broad shoulders in the puffy parka, his shock of white hair, his ruddy cheeks. Everything about him suggested a man who'd had until fifty-eight to achieve what he wanted, a man who'd had all the time in the world. And he was a sportsman. The parka was obviously for skiing.

Arnold's head began to ache.

He had always ordered his life methodically, mathematically, believing absolutely in the power of this approach to yield, if not the best of all possible outcomes, at least the most reasonable. And yet all around him were people like this MacDonald, succeeding haphazardly. Discoveries found in errors, errors pointing to discoveries. Arnold shivered and zipped his coat higher. "Those girls this afternoon," he said.

"Sorry?"

"On the green. Sitting in the sun with their skirts up. I thought you saw them."

MacDonald shook his head. "No. I sat in my office most of the afternoon, but I didn't get much done."

Arnold took a long sip of his coffee and scalded the roof of his mouth. "You were on the library steps. I saw you. The sunlight? On their legs?" He took a deep breath and tried to rein himself in. His head felt heavy, as though he were coming down with something.

"Sorry I missed them," MacDonald said. Then he gave Arnold a big smile. "I haven't seen you in a while. How are you?"

Arnold looked out at the highway. He was tempted to count the cars as he saw them cresting the hill in the distance. When he spoke, he spoke to the horizon. "Working. Working hard." He turned abruptly to MacDonald. "It's going well. I'm just in my forties and have good years left."

"Of course," MacDonald said, puzzled.

"And I'm very near a complete proof of the Riemann Hypothesis."

MacDonald's eyes widened. "I know the Riemann. That's exciting."

Arnold squinted at him. "You shouldn't doubt me."

"I didn't mean—"

"Just this morning I had a breakthrough."

MacDonald stared at him a moment, then smiled. "That's great news." He looked over Arnold's head, lifted his cup, and finished his coffee. "Well, I should get home. Good luck to you."

MacDonald shot his empty cup into the air. It traced a near-perfect arc and dropped squarely into the garbage can several yards away. Arnold shook his head. It was a good shot; amazing, considering the poor aerodynamics of the cup.

Arnold stayed for a time, the twilight descending around him. He counted cars and sipped his coffee. When it was gone, he walked over to the garbage and dropped his cup in. He turned to go but took only a few steps toward his car before he stopped. He looked back over his shoulder at the road behind him. A second later he spun back toward the parking lot.

He couldn't believe what he was seeing.

There was his car directly in front of him, one of many still left in the lot, but beyond it was a prospect identical in all its features to the one behind him. It was perhaps fifty feet to his car, then the parking lot extended the same distance again before the cement balustrade bounded it on the other side. Beyond the balustrade, Arnold could see the pale gray highway, oddly illuminated in the half-dark, stretching to the horizon exactly as it did behind him. To his left and right, approximately forty-five degrees from his forward line of sight, were two identical banks of bathrooms and vending machines. The brown rectangular buildings were parallel to each other and his car was parked at the midpoint between them. At a slightly wider angle, perhaps sixty degrees to either side, he could see the ramps circling up from the highway. They were exactly the same, each with an entrance and an exit.

Which one had he come up?

Arnold's eyes darted back and forth between the ramps and the buildings as around the parking lot yellow fluorescent lights flickered on. He listened to the flush of toilets, the hiss of coffee dispensers, the rumble and crash of soda machines. He no longer felt cold and his excitement was growing. He turned again and looked at the road behind him, scrutinized the gently rolling land divided into a geometric pattern of fields and dotted with bare winter trees. Then he looked back across the parking lot. The landscape was exactly the same. It was impossible to determine from which direction he'd come or which direction was home. The sun had set behind a layer of clouds and both horizons were equally blanched. Everywhere the earth was darker than the sky, and the heavens rose vaulted and radiant over a shadowy world alike in all directions.

He began to grin and lifted himself onto the balls of his feet. He knew what this was. A continuity in space, represented by the symmetrical rest area, was illustrating the ambiguous nature of time, represented by the road. Most people assumed that the arrow of time pointed forward; all scientists knew that this was a convenient description for the world as man had defined it. The trouble was that, mathematically, the relationship between time and space presented a dilemma. Space—x, y, z on the Cartesian plane—was mastered. T, time, remained a mystery. No one knew which way it ran.

Arnold ran across the parking lot.

But what if the road, he realized, thinking fast, everything clicking into place, *was* the arrow of time. By the time he reached the far balustrade and went down on one knee to catch his breath, he knew he was on the verge of something momentous. Panting from his run, the blood pounding in his head, he closed his eyes. He was sweating, he could taste salt and something strangely metallic on his lips, but it was suddenly clear to him that he had discovered the source of the arrow, the origin, the center of time. In one direction from the rest area time was moving forward; in the other, backward.

Still kneeling, he gripped the balustrade with both hands and opened his eyes. He wasn't sure how he'd arrived here, but he was enormously relieved. It solved more than one problem. There was the difficulty with Mary—the impossibility of convincing her, again, to love him; and there was the failure of the Arnold Proof, the error in his calculations he'd seen at the blackboard that morning.

Shaking his head against the memory, Arnold struggled to his feet. But these things lay forward, and now, from here, didn't he have the ability to go backward? Yes! And backward couldn't he find the place where his mathematical ability was graceful and strong, where Mary loved him, and his proof was again within reach? Yes, yes! Of course! All these things still existed, backward. His thoughts were racing. His mind felt sharp and lucid. Mathematics had not abandoned him and everything was making sense again, so much more sense than having spent a mathematician's lifetime on a problem he did not have the ability to solve.

Arnold stood still for a moment and stared straight ahead. But which direction was backward? How would he know which way to go?

He was sure that the answer would come. All the difficulties of the day, all his hard-sought concentration of the past months, had been leading him to this point. Poincaré and his step onto the bus came to mind and he lifted his foot. Suddenly he laughed, a sharp, bleating sound. At this height his foot, small for a man's, blocked out many car headlights. He stuck it out through the balustrade and turned it briskly left and right. This was it, the moment of insight, brief and certain. He'd waited so long.

Acknowledgments

Most of these stories were written while I was living in London and writing each day in the London Library on St. James's Square. I cherish my friends and fellow writers there: Richard Davenport-Hines, Benedict Flynn, Nikki Gemmell, Steve May, John McNally, Giles Milton, Georgina Newbery, John O'Farrell, Christopher Phipps, Anna Reid, and George Tiffin. No writer has ever had a better school. I hope they know how much I miss them, lunches in the square, and pints at the Red Lion.

I am grateful to all my teachers, from the beginning with Jim Melby and David Tabler, to my classes with Frazier Russell and Abby Wender at the Writers Studio in New York City. Many thanks also to Louise Brockett, who gave me my first job in publishing and always encouraged me to keep writing.

I want to thank Robert Wilson and Carol Houck Smith for reading early drafts of several of these stories and offering crucial advice; Dawn Sefarian for her early and strong enthusiasm; Michael Downing and Rachel Cohen for teaching me more about writing and the writing life than they realize; and my brother, Damian, for a perspective on all things that is a fine balance to my own.

I am most grateful to my editor, Jack Shoemaker, and managing editor, Trish Hoard. As colleagues they were forgiving of my writerly ambitions; as publishers, they have been demanding in all the right ways; and as friends, they are without equal.

CPSIA information can be obtained at www.ICGtesting.com
Printed in the USA
LVOW08*0243230813

349275LV00004B/46/A